THE SECOND WORLD WAR
Conflict and co-operation

Sean Lang
Head of History
Hills Road Sixth Form College,
Cambridge

CAMBRIDGE
UNIVERSITY PRESS

Published by the Press Syndicate of the University of Cambridge
The Pitt Building, Trumpington Street, Cambridge CB2 1RP
40 West 20th Street, New York, NY 10011–4211, USA
10 Stamford Road, Oakleigh, Melbourne 3166, Australia

First published 1993

Printed in Great Britain at the University Press, Cambridge.

A catalogue record for this book is available from the British Library.

ISBN 0 521 43826 8 paperback
Designed and produced by Gecko Limited, Bicester, Oxon.
Picture research by Callie Kendall
Illustrations by Nick Asher, Barry Rowe, Martin Sanders and Mel Wright.

Notice to teachers
Many of the sources used in this textbook have been adapted or abridged from the original.

Front cover illustration *'Balloon Site, Coventry'* by Dame Laura Knight,
Imperial War Museum, London.

Acknowledgements

The author and publisher would like to thank the following for permission to use the illustrations on the following pages:

4–5 *background*, 7*tl*, 14, 19, 23 *inset*, 30*l*, 32*r*, 58*t*, 68, 81, 83*t*, Popperfoto; 4, 17*t*, 26-7 *background*, 30*r*, 34*b*, 39, 43, 71, 75*b*, 76, Peter Newark's Military Pictures; 5, *Grief* by Dmitri Baltermants/Novosti Photo Library (London); 6*l*, 12, 15, 20–21 *background*, 22 *inset*, 27 *insets*, 28*t*, 29, 31 *inset*, 32*l*, 59, 34*t*, 35, 37, 45, 52*b*, 57*r*, 59, 64, 73*t*, 78*t*, 79*t*, Imperial War Museum, London; 6*r*, 7*tr*, Mary Evans/Explorer; 7*c*, 36, Mary Evans Picture Library; 7*b*, 17*b*, 31*r*, Robert Hunt Library; 13, 82-3, Ullstein Bilderdienst; 20 *inset*, 28*c*, 52*t*, 53, 56*t*, 58*b*, 84, Topham Picture Source; 21 *inset*, 33, Wiener Library; 24, Camera Press; 25, Archiv für Kunst und Geschichte, Berlin; 40*t*, Bildarchiv Preussisches Kulturbesitz/Arthur Grimm, July 1941; 40*b*, John Heseltine/Robert Hunt Library; 41*t*, 75*t*, Novosti/Robert Hunt Library; 41*b*, 85, Novosti Photo Library (London); 44, David King Collection; 50-51, Rex Features; 56-7 *background*, Wiener Library/©The Auschwitz Museum; 60, Peter Newark's Military Pictures/artist: Roy Nockolds; 61*t*, TRH/NASM; 62, Bildarchiv Preussisches Kulturbesitz/Richard Peter, 1946; 72-3*b*, Panel 34 of the Overlord Embroidery. *The Overlord Embroidery is on permanent display at the D-Day Museum, Portsmouth*; 74, Sygma/©Keystone; 78-9*b*, USAF/Ann Ronan at Image Select; 80, TRH/DOD; 86, National Museum of Labour History; 87, Michael George/Impact Photos; 90, 91, UPI/Bettmann Archive; 92-3*t*, 93*r*, Associated Press/Topham Picture Library; 92*b*, Zefa-Streichen; 93*b*, Vincent Bunce.

CONTENTS

INTRODUCTION: TOTAL WAR

The Second World War lasted from 1939 to 1945: it was the largest war the world has ever endured. It was fought over six continents, and more than 50 million men, women and children were killed. Civilians were as heavily involved as soldiers, sailors and airmen: it was total war.

Why did the Second World War begin?

Nuremberg Rally

It was the terrifying evil of fascism that sparked off the war. At mass rallies like this one, Nazi Germans were taught to hate their neighbours and to fight to control the world.

Hiroshima

New advances in physics meant that the Americans were able to develop the atom bomb. For the first time in history it was possible to destroy an entire city in a matter of seconds. To help end the war, atom bombs were dropped twice, completely devastating the Japanese cities of Hiroshima and Nagasaki.

Areas of conflict during the Second World War.

The world at war

Although the war began as a quarrel between the nations of Europe, it soon involved the colonies and dominions of Europe across the world. From the snows of Russia to the deserts of Somalia, from the Canadian forests to the jungles of Papua New Guinea, there was hardly a corner of the world whose people were not affected by the war.

Civilian casualties

In this war between industrialised nations, factories, shipyards and mines were targets just as much as fortresses and airfields were. Thousands of people were killed in bombing raids on cities, and in Europe and Asia, millions of civilians were worked to death or simply murdered in appalling slave labour camps. Civilians also died at sea when passenger ships were torpedoed, and huge numbers of civilians perished when battles raged through towns and cities.

What happened during those years of world conflict?

1 Democracy and dictatorship

In the 1930s there was a war in Abyssinia, civil war in Spain, and serious street fighting in Britain.

What was all this fighting about?

In each case the argument was about *power*. People disagreed violently about how governments should be organised. There were three main types of government in the 1930s: *democracy*, *fascism*, and *communism*.

U.S.A.

Franklin Roosevelt.

General Franco.

...ville Chamberlain.

GREAT
BRITAIN

Joseph Stalin.

SOVIET UNION

Adolf Hitler.

FRANCE

ITALY

SPAIN

Benito Mussolini.

Type of government
DEMOCRACY

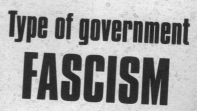

Origins Originally started with the ancient Greeks. Developed gradually in western Europe and America in the nineteenth century.

Beliefs People have the right to elect their government and to say what they like. There are different political parties, and newspapers are not controlled by the government.

Examples in the 1930s Great Britain, Czechoslovakia, France, United States.

Comments The democratic countries had parliaments and allowed anyone to speak or write freely. Unfortunately, free speech and elections were not enough to solve the economic depression that hit the world in the 1930s.

Key individuals
Franklin Roosevelt - *President of United States.*
Winston Churchill - *Prime Minister of Great Britain.*

Type of government
FASCISM

Origins Started when Mussolini took control in Italy in 1922. 'Fascist' comes from the word *fasces*, which was a symbol of government in ancient Rome.

Beliefs The state should have a strong leader, a *dictator*, and everyone should obey him. Fascist governments destroyed other political parties and controlled the media. Fascists hated trade unions, Communists and different *ethnic groups* such as the German Jews.

Examples in the 1930s Italy, Nazi Germany, Spain.

Comments Fascist leaders promised jobs; they also mounted huge displays, with uniforms and special salutes. They did not allow anyone to oppose them, and many of the jobs they provided came from making armaments.

Key individuals
Adolf Hitler - *Fascist dictator of Germany.*
Benito Mussolini - *Fascist dictator of Italy.*
General Franco - *Fascist dictator of Spain.*

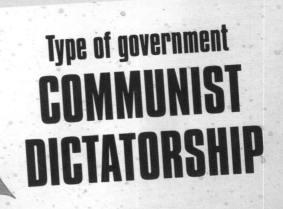

Type of government
COMMUNIST DICTATORSHIP

Origins The Russian Revolution of 1917 was the beginning of the world's first communist state.

Beliefs The Communist Party should run the country on behalf of the working people, the proletariat. Other parties and non-communist newspapers should be destroyed. All factories and other work-places should be controlled by the government.

Examples in the 1930s Soviet Union.

Comments The Russian Revolution was led by Lenin, Trotsky and Stalin. Stalin took control of the Communist Party when Lenin died. He made all communists throughout the world do as he said. He was terrified of enemies in the Communist Party, so he had thousands of people in the Soviet Union, including many leading communists, arrested and executed.

Key individual
Joseph Stalin - Communist dictator of the Soviet Union.

1 a Say which of the following countries were fascist, communist or democratic in the 1930s: Spain, Soviet Union, France, United States, Great Britain, Germany.
b Explain in your own words which one of the three systems of government gave people the most freedom.

2 a How would a communist be treated under each system of government?
b What similarities and differences are there between fascism and communism?

1919: Treaty of Versailles

At the end of the First World War, Germany had to sign the Treaty of Versailles which forced her to give up land and to pay a huge sum of money. A League of Nations was set up to safeguard world peace, but without American help the League was not strong enough to stop aggressive nations.

1922: Mussolini seizes power in Italy

Mussolini and his fascist followers, known as 'blackshirts', marched on Rome and seized power in Italy. Mussolini became *Il Duce* ('the Leader') and set up an efficient but brutal rule over Italy. Soon Mussolini was demanding more land for Italy.

1927: Stalin seizes power in Russia

After a terrible civil war and famine, in which millions of Russians died, Stalin ('Man of Steel') took power in the Soviet Union. He immediately started putting his opponents to death, and began a ruthless programme to build up industry in the Soviet Union, killing anyone who stood in his way.

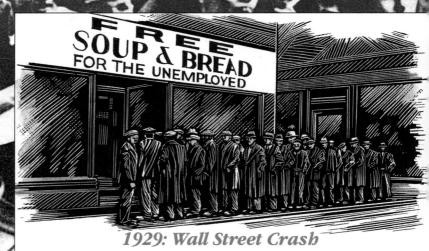

1929: Wall Street Crash

A great economic depression struck the world in 1929 and continued throughout the 1930s. There was mass unemployment with over 2 million in Great Britain, 6 million in Germany, and 15 million in the United States out of work.

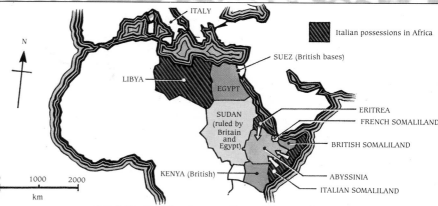

1935: Italy invades Abyssinia

Mussolini wanted to set up a new Roman Empire, so he began by attacking Abyssinia (modern Ethiopia). Using aircraft and poison gas, the Italians soon overcame the poorly-equipped Abyssinians. When the League of Nations protested at this aggression, Mussolini simply left the League.

1933: Hitler takes power in Germany

When Adolf Hitler promised Germans he would tear up the Treaty of Versailles, he won the elections and became Chancellor of Germany. He quickly gathered all power in his own hands and began arresting communists, trade unionists and Jews.

1938: Germany invades Austria and Czechoslovakia

Hitler met a warm welcome when he led his troops into Austria, but the Czech government seemed prepared to fight when he tried to take over the Sudetenland, an area of Czechoslovakia. However, when Britain and France told the Czechs to hand the areas over, the Czechs had to give in. The next year, Hitler took over the rest of Czechoslovakia.

1936: Spanish Civil War

In 1936, civil war broke out in Spain between the Republicans and General Franco's Nationalists. Mussolini and Hitler sent men and aircraft to help Franco. Stalin sent money to help the Republicans. After two years of bitter fighting, Franco won the war and took control in Spain.

2 Germany prepares for war

The Treaty of Versailles, which was signed at the end of the First World War, was supposed to keep a firm check on Germany. By 1938 Germany had seized land from many of her neighbours and was still demanding more.

Why did Germany bring Europe to the edge of war?

To make sense of why war began in Europe in 1939 we need to know how Hitler came to power in the 1930s and why the other European countries failed to stand up to Hitler's Germany. In the 1960s the historian A.J.P. Taylor surprised many people when he wrote a book suggesting that the roots of the war lay deep in German history. In particular he saw a link between the end of the First World War and the start of the Second World War.

Source A

'The Second World War was, in large part, a repeat performance of the first.... . Germany fought specifically in the Second World War to reverse the verdict of the first and to destroy the settlement which followed it.... . The first war explains the second and, in fact, caused it.'

A.J.P. Taylor, *The Origins of the Second World War*, 1961

To understand what Taylor meant, we need to know how the First World War ended, and what Germans thought about it.

How the Germans saw Versailles

Many Germans felt that the terms of the dictated 'peace' of Versailles were unacceptable.

The treaty stated that Germany must:
- give up huge areas of national land
- give up all colonies overseas
- reduce its army to only 100,000 men
- reduce its navy and scrap its submarines
- scrap all its air force
- pay a vast sum of money (called *reparations*) to the French and British.

Above all, the treaty claimed that
- the Great War was *all Germany's fault!*

Source B

A poster produced for the 1932 German election. 'We farmers are mucking out. We vote National Socialist (Nazi Party).'
- *The other people shown on the poster represent communists and Jewish financiers. What do you think is meant by 'mucking out'?*

12

If you had been at school in Nazi Germany, you would certainly have learnt about the Treaty of Versailles, like the girl who wrote this for her homework.

Source C

'We pay and pay to France, and borrow and borrow from America. The Rhine and the Ruhr are saved, but you will pay until you drop. From 1918 to 1988, pay, pay, pay, pay, pay: father, son, grandson, great-grandson, great-great-grandson.'

Vote for Hitler!

For Germans, things got worse in the 1920s. Their money became worthless; a French army occupied the Ruhr, Germany's industrial region; and they still had to pay the huge reparations bill to the Allies. By 1932 things were even worse. The Americans could not afford to send more money to support German industry, and thousands of Germans were out of work.

1932 was election year. The Nazi Party made a set of very attractive promises:

- Tear up the Treaty of Versailles.
- Build up the armed forces.
- Work for all.
- Reunite the Fatherland.

The Nazis also said that the Jews were to blame for Germany's problems. Brown-shirted Nazi thugs, the SA, beat up Jews in the streets.

The Nazis won the 1932 elections and in January 1933 their leader, Adolf Hitler, became Chancellor (Prime Minister) of Germany. Almost immediately, he started to take over other areas of Europe and to defy the Treaty of Versailles.

Source D

Hitler becoming Chancellor in January 1933.

Appeasement

In the late 1930s Britain and France followed a policy of *appeasement*. This meant giving in to Germany's demands in order to prevent a war. The British, led by their Prime Minister Neville Chamberlain, thought that the Treaty of Versailles was unfair anyway, and they would not fight a war to enforce it; the French liked the treaty, but they would not do anything without the British. You can see the areas the Germans took over on the map.

The hardest test for appeasement was when Hitler demanded that part of Czechoslovakia called the Sudetenland. The Czechs were allied to France and seemed ready to fight. To stop this, Chamberlain, Mussolini and the French Prime Minister all travelled to meet Hitler at Munich in September 1938. There they all agreed to hand the Sudetenland over to Germany. Deserted by their allies, the Czechs had no choice but to give in.

Source E

Chamberlain on his return from Munich on 30 September 1938 telling the crowd that there would be 'Peace in our time'.

● *Explain what he meant by the phrase 'Peace in our time'.*

Source F

'You only have to look at the map to see that nothing that France or Britain could do could possibly save Czechoslovakia from being overrun by the Germans, if they wanted to do it.'

Neville Chamberlain's diary, 20 March 1938

Saarland: voted to rejoin Germany in 1935
Rhineland: German troops invaded in 1936
Austria: taken over by Germany (the *Anschluss*) in 1938
Sudetenland: occupied by Germany in 1938
Czechoslovakia: Germany invaded in 1939
Poland: invaded by Germany and Soviet Union in 1939
Danzig Corridor: claimed by Germany in 1939

This map of Europe shows the expansion of Germany before the outbreak of the war.

War

Things hotted up in 1939. In March, Hitler suddenly took over the rest of Czechoslovakia. In August he signed a non-aggression pact with, of all people, Stalin. This said that the Soviet Union and Nazi Germany would work together and would not go to war with each other. They also agreed to carve up Poland between them. Hitler then started demanding land around the port of Danzig from Poland.

Source G

A cartoonist's view of the pact between Hitler and Stalin showing the dictators marching together.
Why do you think each is shown with a hand on his gun?

This time Britain and France stood firm. On 1 September 1939, Germany invaded Poland without warning. Two days later, Britain and France declared war on Germany.

---

1 Explain why many Germans were very bitter about the Treaty of Versailles.

2 Why were the Nazi election promises of 1932 attractive to many Germans?

3 What was 'appeasement'? Why do you think it failed to stop the war?

4 In Source A, A.J.P. Taylor suggested that the end of the First World War was the key cause of the Second World War. Using all the evidence from this unit, do you agree with him?

3 Blitzkrieg

Instead of years of weary slogging in trenches, as in the First World War, Britain and France were beaten back quickly and it seemed the war would be all over in a matter of months.

Why were the Germans so successful in the early days of the war?

A new type of attack

Secret German war plans were code-named after colours. The plan to attack Poland was called *Plan White*. It was to be a new type of attack, and it became known as *Blitzkrieg* (lightning war).

In a Blitzkrieg speed was vital. The idea was to create panic and confusion as quickly as possible.

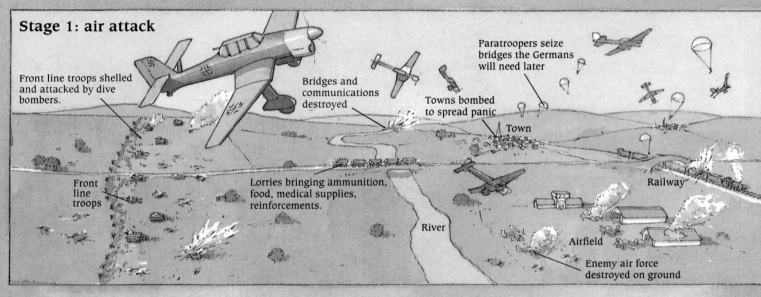

Stage 1: air attack

Front line troops shelled and attacked by dive bombers.

Bridges and communications destroyed

Paratroopers seize bridges the Germans will need later

Towns bombed to spread panic

Town

Front line troops

Lorries bringing ammunition, food, medical supplies, reinforcements.

Railway

River

Airfield

Enemy air force destroyed on ground

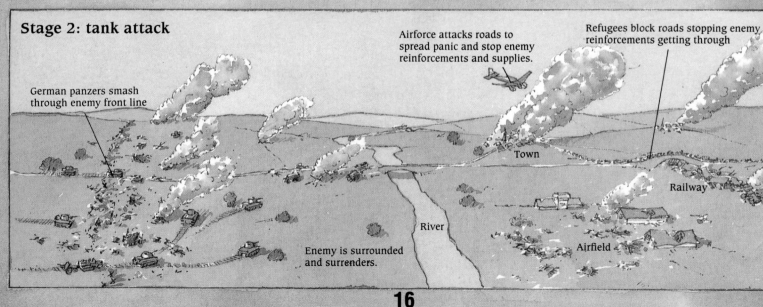

Stage 2: tank attack

Airforce attacks roads to spread panic and stop enemy reinforcements and supplies.

Refugees block roads stopping enemy reinforcements getting through

German panzers smash through enemy front line

Town

Railway

River

Airfield

Enemy is surrounded and surrenders.

How Blitzkrieg worked

Plan White was a devastating success. On 1 September 1939, without any warning, German tanks (*panzers*) tore the Polish army to pieces. The roads were so badly clogged with refugees that the Polish tanks could not get through, and the Poles had to send their cavalry in against the panzers. The horses stood no chance against the German tanks. Soon the Poles were forced back to their capital, Warsaw.

Source A

The JU87 Stuka dive bomber was specially equipped with sirens to make its bombing attacks even more terrifying by spreading panic among the refugees trying to escape the advancing tanks and troops.

There, they were able to put up a stronger fight, and German casualties were high in their attack on Warsaw. But on 17 September disaster struck for the Poles: the Russians invaded Poland from the east. Caught between two huge armies, the Poles were forced to surrender.

Source B

Panzers (tanks) were an essential part of the Blitzkrieg.

Source C

A Polish officer who saw the Blitzkrieg remembered the German attack as an old man.

'We were a good cavalry regiment, able to fight infantry or cavalry, not German tanks. So the horses were used as quick transport and we fought as infantry. One-third of the soldiers had to stay with the horses; only two-thirds actually fought.

Virtually total air superiority allowed the Germans to penetrate the country deep beyond the front line.'

Jozef Garlinski, 1989

NORWAY

DENMARK

GREAT BRITAIN

KEY
German conquests

1 Poland – September 1939

2 Denmark and Norway –
  April – June 1940

3 Holland, Belgium,
  Luxembourg and France –
  May – June 1940

Germany, September
1939

German conquests,
September 1939 –
June 1940

HOLLAND

BELGIUM

LUX

POLAND

FRANCE

The beginning of the war in Europe.
The first German conquests.

A Phoney War?

Meanwhile, in the west, nothing much seemed to be happening. The French sat behind a huge line of fortresses called the *Maginot line*. People nicknamed all the waiting around 'sitzkrieg' or the *Phoney War*. When the Germans eventually attacked they went around the Maginot line.

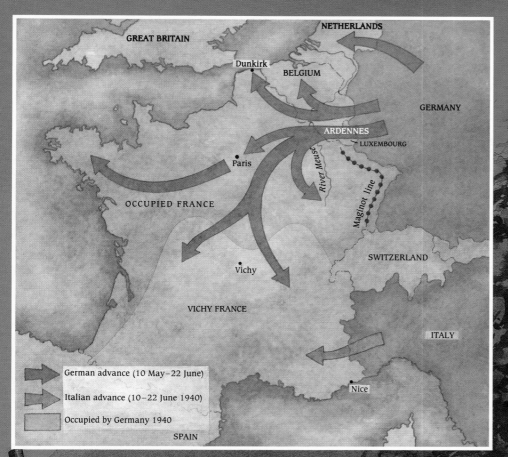

The German invasion of France and the Low Countries, 1940.

Key:
- German advance (10 May–22 June)
- Italian advance (10–22 June 1940)
- Occupied by Germany 1940

Hitler strikes to the north and west

On 9 April 1940, German troops tore through Denmark and landed in Norway. British and French troops managed to hold on to the port of Narvik for a time, and they sank ten German destroyers, but it was not enough: the Germans took control of Norway.

In Britain, people were furious. Chamberlain was forced to resign, and on 10 May Winston Churchill became Prime Minister. But that same day disaster struck again. German troops smashed their way into Belgium and The Netherlands. *Plan Yellow*, the long-awaited German attack in the west, had begun.

The Belgians surrendered quickly, but there was fierce resistance in The Netherlands before the Dutch surrendered.

Source D

Winston Churchill became the British Prime Minister after the fall of Norway.

Dunkirk

However, the main German attack was yet to come. It came through the forest of the Ardennes, where French defences were weak. German panzers raced across to the Channel coast and cut the Allied armies off from the rest of France. The Allies were forced back to the port of Dunkirk. And then the Germans did a very strange thing. They stopped.

The order to stop came from Hitler. We are still not sure why he gave it, but it gave the British time to launch *Operation Dynamo*: hundreds of ships and boats of all sizes, even pleasure craft, were sent across the Channel to rescue 300,000 British and French troops from the beaches at Dunkirk. The troops had to leave all their tanks and heavy guns behind, so although Operation Dynamo became known as 'the miracle of Dunkirk', really the Allies had been soundly beaten.

Source E

Withdrawal from Dunkirk, *by Charles Cundall, shows the evacuation of Dunkirk between 27 May and 4 June 1940 by an 'armada' of boats including pleasure boats, fishing smacks and naval vessels.*

France defeated

On 14 June, German troops entered Paris and a week later France surrendered. The Germans forced the French to sign the surrender in the same place where the Germans had been made to surrender in 1918. France was to be divided in two. The northern half was to be occupied by Germany; the southern half was to be governed by Marshal Pétain, and became known as *Vichy France*. Pétain had been a French hero in the First World War, but now he had to learn to work with the Nazis.

Source F

German victory parade in Paris.

Charles Cundall 1940

Source G

Checkmate! Schach dem King! *A German propaganda cartoon from 1940 showing the King of England George VI in the last corner of the chess board surrounded by a Stuka dive-bomber, a paratrooper, a panzer tank and a U-boat. Chamberlain lies flat out while Churchill is fleeing.*

● *How did the cartoonist think the war was going for both sides?*

1 Look carefully at the diagram on page 16 and then explain in your own words how Blitzkrieg worked.

2 a What reasons can you find in Source C for the Germans' success in Poland?
b How many of these reasons are also shown in Source G? What other reasons does Source G give?

3 Why do you think the British called Dunkirk 'a miracle'? Were they right?

4 Why do you think that by June 1940 many people thought Germany was going to win the war?

5 Using information from this unit, explain why the Germans were so successful in the early days of the war.

4 Britain embattled

'In six weeks, Britain will have her neck wrung like a chicken,' predicted a French leader in June 1940. At this time Britain was fighting virtually alone against a triumphant Germany. Britain seemed to face certain defeat.

How did Britain survive against the might of Germany?

The Battle of Britain

Hitler expected Britain to surrender after the fall of France, and he was surprised when Churchill refused to do so. Hastily, his generals drew up a plan to invade Britain. It was code-named *Operation Sealion*. It would mean crossing the Channel in the face of the powerful Royal Navy, so the Germans had to control the air above the Channel. Hermann Goering, the leader of the German air force, the *Luftwaffe*, promised to win control of the skies from the Royal Air Force. The defeat of the RAF would be the signal for an invasion of Britain.

1940 *August*

- German Luftwaffe attacks RAF airfields in southern England, but suffers heavy losses.
- RAF *Spitfires* and *Hurricanes* are guided to their targets by *radar* (*ra*dio *d*etection *a*nd *r*anging), but suffer badly from attacks on their airfields and on radar stations.

1940 *September*

- Luftwaffe starts heavy bombing over London, which allows the RAF and radar stations to recover.
- Heavy Luftwaffe losses force Hitler to postpone Operation Sealion. Later he abandons it altogether.

The RAF pilots who fought in the Battle of Britain became known as 'The Few', after Winston Churchill honoured their victory with this speech:

'Never in the field of human conflict was so much owed by so many to so few.'

Source A

RAF pilots 'scramble' to their aircraft to intercept the approaching enemy aircraft.

British fighter planes attacking a German bomber formation. This modern illustration shows a Heinkel III bomber formation with Messerschmitt ME109 fighter escort being attacked by Spitfires.

Source B

Women in operations room. When radar detected Luftwaffe bombers approaching, operations rooms like this directed the RAF fighter squadrons to intercept the enemy formations.

Source C

German pilot and navigator inside a Heinkel III.

It was a very close-run thing. By the end, the pilots on both sides were exhausted. What saved the RAF was the Luftwaffe's decision to start bombing London. The Germans had lost the 'Battle of Britain' – this made an invasion in 1940 impossible.

Source D

A Heinkel III on a bombing raid over London.

Source E

Richard Hillary, an RAF pilot, describes his experience in the Battle of Britain:

'The voice of the controller came unhurried over the loud-speaker, telling us to take off, and in a few seconds we were running for our machines. I climbed into the cockpit of my plane and felt an empty feeling in my stomach. For one second time seemed to stand still and I stared blankly in front of me. I knew that that morning I was to kill for the first time. That I might be killed or in any way injured did not occur to me. I knew it could not happen to me. I suppose every pilot knows that it cannot happen to him: even when he is taking off for the last time, when he will not return, he knows that he cannot be killed. Then I was being strapped in, my mind checking the controls, and we were off.

We ran into them at 18,000 feet, twenty yellow-nosed Messerschmitt 109s, about 500 feet above us. Our squadron strength was eight, and as they came down we turned head on into them. . . I saw Brian let go a burst of fire at the leading plane, saw the pilot put his machine in a half roll and knew that he was mine. I turned the gun button to 'fire' and let go a 4-second burst. He came right through my sights and I saw the tracer from all eight guns thud home. For a second he seemed to hang in the air; then a jet of flame shot upwards and he spun out of sight...'

(Richard Hillary was later killed in action on 7 July 1943.)

The Battle of the Atlantic

Winston Churchill called the struggle to control the Atlantic the most important battle of the war. Britain depended heavily on importing food and oil from abroad, and it had to come by sea. The Germans sent submarines, called U-boats, to sink the ships. Hitler knew that he did not need to invade Britain. He could win the war by starving the British people into submission.

The ships stood a better chance when they sailed in groups called convoys, protected by naval escorts. The escort ships used Asdic, a sort of underwater radar, to find the U-boats, and depth charges to attack them. Even so, the U-boats were able to sink huge numbers of ships. It was not until 1943 that the tide began to turn: the Americans developed long-range aircraft that could hunt the U-boats far out in the Atlantic, and a new improved depth charge made it much easier for convoys to defend themselves.

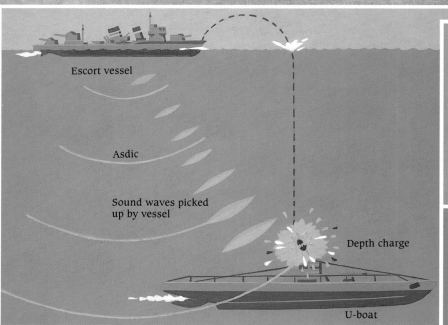

Asdic produces a sound echo revealing the enemy's position. Depth charges large explosive devices set to explode at the submarine's estimated depth, are then used to crush the pressure hull of the submarine.

Allied shipping losses in tons

Year	Tons
1941	4,100,000
1942	7,700,000
1943	2,900,000
1944	750,000
1945	250,000

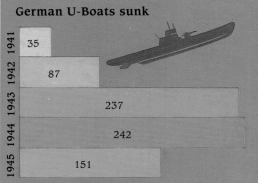

German U-Boats sunk

Year	Number
1941	35
1942	87
1943	237
1944	242
1945	151

Source F

A German U-boat shells a merchant ship, from a painting by H. R. Butler.

A FEW CARELESS WORDS MAY END IN THIS—

Source G

A propaganda poster showing the sinking of a merchant ship. Many posters in the Second World War had similar warnings about careless talk. Can you explain why?

Source H

Convoys could also be attacked by surface raiders like the German battleship Bismarck. *In this painting by John Hamilton the* Bismarck *is being torpedoed by British aircraft during the Battle of the Atlantic in May 1941.*

Soon afterwards it was sunk by Royal Navy ships. The Bismarck *was unsuccessful as a surface raider – it had never attacked a convoy.*

The Desert War

Towards the end of the Battle of Britain in 1940, Mussolini ordered his troops to attack British possessions in Africa. The British threw the Italians out and then invaded the Italians' own colonies, Abyssinia and Libya. 100,000 Italians, including six generals, surrendered.

The Germans were alarmed, and sent a large army, the *Afrika Korps*, under Field Marshal Rommel, to help the Italians. Rommel drove the British back, and in June 1942 he captured 25,000 Commonwealth troops at Tobruk.

Rommel felt encouraged to attack the British base in Egypt. The British commander, General Montgomery, was expecting the attack, and defeated Rommel in a massive battle at *El Alamein* in October 1942.

Source I

Field Marshal Rommel, known to his enemies as 'the Desert Fox'.

Source J

General Montgomery.

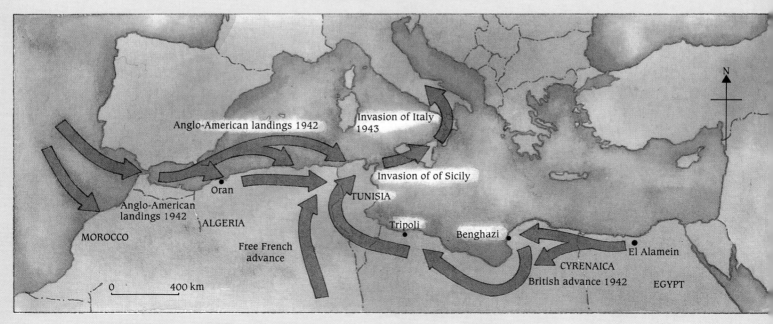

The war in North Africa and the Mediterranean, 1942 – 43.

Source K

Australian infantry attack at El Alamein.

Source L

A poster issued to show how all parts of the Empire gave support to Britain. Jewish, African, or West Indian troops who fought for Britain could expect little mercy from the Germans if they were captured.

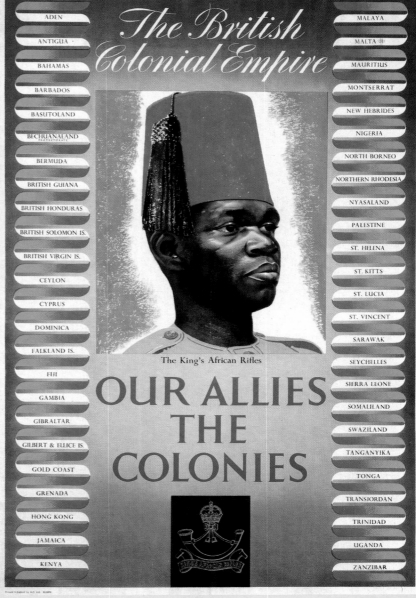

The British Colonial Empire

ADEN
ANTIGUA
BAHAMAS
BARBADOS
BASUTOLAND
BECHUANALAND PROTECTORATE
BERMUDA
BRITISH GUIANA
BRITISH HONDURAS
BRITISH SOLOMON IS.
BRITISH VIRGIN IS.
CEYLON
CYPRUS
DOMINICA
FALKLAND IS.
FIJI
GAMBIA
GIBRALTAR
GILBERT & ELLICE IS.
GOLD COAST
GRENADA
HONG KONG
JAMAICA
KENYA

MALAYA
MALTA
MAURITIUS
MONTSERRAT
NEW HEBRIDES
NIGERIA
NORTH BORNEO
NORTHERN RHODESIA
NYASALAND
PALESTINE
ST. HELENA
ST. KITTS
ST. LUCIA
ST. VINCENT
SARAWAK
SEYCHELLES
SIERRA LEONE
SOMALILAND
SWAZILAND
TANGANYIKA
TONGA
TRANSJORDAN
TRINIDAD
UGANDA
ZANZIBAR

The King's African Rifles

OUR ALLIES THE COLONIES

---

1 Look at this list of reasons why Germany lost the Battle of Britain. Explain in your own words how each reason made a difference to the outcome of the battle.

◆ The British had radar.
◆ The Germans started bombing London.
◆ The Germans miscalculated how many RAF planes they shot down.

Can you add any reasons of your own to explain why Germany lost the Battle of Britain?

2 a What was the Battle of the Atlantic?
b Why do you think Churchill considered it the most important battle of the war for Britain?

3 How successful was Britain in fighting the Desert War?

5 The Home Front in Britain

On 14 November 1940 German bombers destroyed the centre of the medieval city of Coventry. Joseph Goebbels, the German Propaganda Minister, wrote in his diary that there was 'total helplessness in London. A great wave of pessimism there'.

Was he right? How united was Britain?

As more and more men went away to war, extra help was desperately needed in the factories and on the farms, so women were called up to work in industry, or to join the Women's Land Army and help feed the nation.

Source A
Women labouring in a steelworks.

Source C
Dig for Victory. People were encouraged to grow food on every available piece of land.

Source B

Wynne Bates joined the Women's Auxiliary Air Force (the WAAF) and trained as an electrician.

'We were met with absolute hostility. Until then, only men had been doing our jobs and they laughed at us women in big dungarees climbing up and seeing to the generators.'

quoted in *The Independent*, 1991

Rationing

Food and clothes were in very short supply and had to be rationed, so it was important to be economical in cooking and shopping. Different goods, like vegetables and fruit, came on and off the ration according to how available they were. People with lots of money could buy more than their ration from black-market traders known as 'spivs'.

Invasion?

In 1940 the Channel Islands fell to the Germans, and if the RAF lost the Battle of Britain, there was a danger that the Germans would land in England. Volunteers joined the *Home Guard* to man road blocks and to practise blowing up tanks. The Home Guard was mostly made up of old men, and to start with they had no uniforms or weapons, so it was just as well the Germans never actually landed!

Air raids

The biggest danger came from air raids. Whole areas of the City of London and the docklands were destroyed by German bombers in the *Blitz*. Other big cities like Birmingham, Liverpool, Bristol, Glasgow, Plymouth, Belfast, Newcastle and Manchester were heavily bombed too. Dover was shelled from across the Channel in Calais.

In 1942 the RAF bombed the historic German town of Lübeck, and in revenge the Luftwaffe bombed a number of historic towns like Exeter, York, Canterbury, Bath and Norwich, to try to damage British *morale*.

To confuse the bombers, the government imposed a *blackout*. Windows had to be covered with heavy black material, and car headlamps were cut down to tiny slits of light.

Factories often had large underground air raid shelters for their workers, or they used the basements of big hotels and department stores, and in London people also used the Underground.

For the most part, heavy bombing merely made people more determined to win. But not surprisingly, people did sometimes get depressed and fed up with spending each night in cramped shelters.

Source D

People sleeping in the Underground to avoid the bombs.

Source E

The London Blitz. Fire rages after another air raid on London in 1940.

Evacuation

There was no complete protection from air raids. When war broke out, children were evacuated from the big cities. Some went to Canada and America, until the ships carrying them began to be torpedoed. Most went to the country. For some children it was a great adventure, but many felt homesick and came home again.

Source F

Not all evacuees had an easy time when they reached the country.

'They unloaded us on the corner of the street, we thought it was all arranged, but it wasn't. The billeting officer walked along knocking on doors and asked if they'd take a family. We were the last to be picked. You couldn't blame them; they didn't have any coloured people there in those days.'

Quoted in Caroline Lang, *Keep Smiling Through*, 1989

Source G

A group of evacuees.

Source H

A London bus in a crater. Photographs like this were censored by the government.

● *Why?*

---

1 Look carefully at all the sources in this chapter. For each one, say whether it is evidence of *unity* or *disunity* in Britain. (There may be some that are neither.)

2 Some of the photographs in this chapter were carefully posed to give a good impression. Which ones? Do you think they are still useful to us in learning about the war?

3 Suppose you were a German spy in Britain. Using *all* the evidence in this chapter, write a report for Goebbels showing that he was right about what it was like in Britain. (You might need to twist some of the evidence!)

4 Some historians feel that British people were united in this period, while others feel that it was a period of great disunity. How can historians come to such different conclusions?

6 Life under Hitler

Hitler said he wanted a 'New Order' in Europe, a new, strong German Reich (Empire) that would last a thousand years.

What was life like in Hitler's Germany?

Growing up in Nazi Germany

The photograph in Source A shows a Nazi family in uniform. The girl is in the uniform of the League of German Maidens, and the two boys are members of the Hitler Youth. All children in Nazi Germany were supposed to join these organisations. Other youth groups, like the Scouts and Guides, were banned.

Hitler Youth members swore loyalty to Hitler, the *Führer* (Leader), and paraded with drums and flags. At weekends there were hikes and camps in the countryside. It was all very good preparation for life in the army. At school, lessons and textbooks gave only the Nazi point of view. History lessons said how glorious Germany had been in the past and how unfair the Treaty of Versailles was. Everything bad was blamed on the Jews, and teachers encouraged pupils to hate the Jewish children in their class.

The Nazis did not have everything their own way. Sometimes Hitler Youth patrols in the countryside were beaten up by gangs of rebellious teenagers called 'Edelweiss Pirates'.

Even so, opposing the Nazis was very dangerous. It was only too easy to be arrested and sent to a concentration camp because of something you said or because of who your friends were. Even if you were released from the concentration camp, as some people were, memories of the beatings and the lack of food were enough to keep most people quiet.

Source A

A Nazi family photograph.

33

The treatment of women

All the powerful Nazis were men and they had a very narrow idea of how women should spend their lives. They talked about the three Ks: *Kinder*, *Kirche* and *Küche* (Children, Church and Kitchen); by this they meant that a woman's job was to be a mother, go to church and do the cooking.

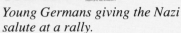

Source B
Young Germans giving the Nazi salute at a rally.

Source C
This poster from 1938 promotes the Nazi view of ideal youth and encourages young people to be involved with the Nazi cause.

Source D
Goebbels, the Nazi head of propaganda, did not think that women should go out to work.

'Woman has the job of being beautiful and bringing children into the world. Like a female bird she should preen herself for her mate and hatch her eggs for him.'

Joseph Goebbels, 1934

Once they were in power, the Nazis began to stop women from doing better-paid jobs. Married women doctors and civil servants all lost their jobs. Women were not allowed to be judges. Courses in schools for girls were changed to put more emphasis on cooking and sewing and less on the qualifications needed for well-paid jobs.

Good times, bad times

Life in Nazi Germany could be pleasant. There were cheap holidays for working people arranged by the 'Strength through Joy' movement, and plenty of work making weapons or helping bring in the harvest. The war news was very good, at least to start with, and if you were in the forces there was the chance of a posting somewhere pleasant like Paris or Brussels.

The German secret police, the *Gestapo*, controlled the occupied countries through terror. Newspapers and radio were censored, and no one was allowed out at night. Anyone caught listening to the BBC or writing anti-German graffiti would be sent to a concentration camp.

Collaborators

In many countries people were prepared to help or *collaborate* with the Germans, and in all the occupied countries, plenty of people even volunteered to join the *Schutzstaffel*, or SS, which was a special Nazi army unit noted for its ruthlessness.

The Norwegian Nazi leader was called Vidkun Quisling. 'Quisling' became a nickname for people in any country who helped the Germans.

Source E

A recruiting poster encouraging people in occupied Denmark to join the SS.

Problems

Many Germans only really began to worry when the RAF began to bomb Berlin in August 1940. Hermann Goering had boasted that no enemy plane could ever drop bombs on Berlin, so the British raids came as a dreadful shock.

Source F

The Nazi Minister of Propaganda noted a change of mood in his diary.

'Morale slightly lower at home. Our people have to first accustom themselves to the thought of a second winter at war. I am receiving a whole series of complaining letters. We must conduct our propaganda more intensely and with more skill.'

Joseph Goebbels, October 1940

● What might the Germans have been complaining about?

The Germans were taken by surprise when they lost the Battle of Britain. It meant the war would not be over as quickly as they had hoped.

The British were also blockading German ports so that food supplies could not get in. Soon the Germans had to start rationing food and clothing. They even had to ration bread, which was never rationed in Britain during the war.

Life under German occupation

What about people in the countries that were taken over by the Germans? What was life like for them?

In some ways, life went on as normal. People still had to go to work, to school or to the shops, and all of these meant having to work with the Germans, because only they could issue identity cards, ration books and work permits.

The Germans needed people to work in their factories so they forced people in occupied countries to travel to Germany to work. In the Channel Islands, the Germans shipped everyone who had been born in Britain to Germany as forced labour. Forced labour workers were treated virtually as slaves, forced to work until they died from exhaustion.

Source G
Joseph Goebbels.

ILS DONNENT LEUR SANG

DONNEZ VOTRE TRAVAIL

pour sauver l'Europe du Bolchevisme

Source H

A French poster calling for volunteers to work in Germany. As the war progressed people were forced to go and work in Germany.

● *Why do you think there was a change from volunteer to forced labour?*

Resistance

Until the end of the war, very few people in occupied countries were prepared to fight against the Germans. The Germans were good at recruiting spies to get inside resistance groups and report back to the Gestapo.

If the Germans could not catch resistance fighters, they took *reprisals* against innocent people. In 1942 Czech resistance fighters killed Reinhard Heydrich, the brutal head of the German secret police in Czechoslovakia. In revenge, the Germans picked at random a village called Lidice, and killed everyone in it. Then they burnt all the buildings and removed the village's name from maps and signposts.

1 a How did the Nazis try to make sure that young German people believed in Hitler's ideas?
b Can you find any evidence in this unit that the Nazis were not completely successful in their work with young people?

2 What information in this unit suggests that
a some people enjoyed aspects of life in Hitler's Germany

b some people were badly treated in Hitler's Germany?

3 In what ways did life become harder for German people as the war went on?

4 How can you explain the fact that people ruled by Hitler had very different opinions about him?

7 The Russian Front

The Soviet Union was a mighty power, with the largest army in the world, yet when the Germans attacked in 1941 they took the Russians by surprise and nearly reached the gates of Moscow.

Why was the Soviet Union so badly prepared for the war?

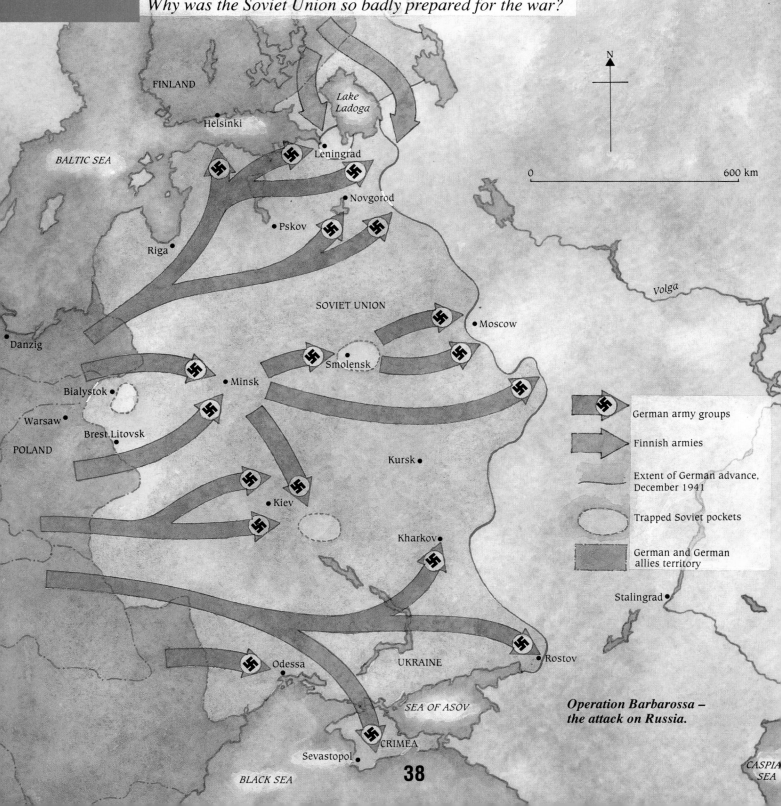

FINLAND

Helsinki

Lake Ladoga

N

BALTIC SEA

0   600 km

Leningrad

Novgorod

Riga

Pskov

Danzig

Volga

SOVIET UNION

Smolensk

Moscow

Bialystok

Minsk

Warsaw

POLAND

Brest Litovsk

Kursk

Kiev

Kharkov

German army groups

Finnish armies

Extent of German advance, December 1941

Trapped Soviet pockets

German and German allies territory

Stalingrad

Odessa

UKRAINE

Rostov

SEA OF ASOV

Operation Barbarossa – the attack on Russia.

CRIMEA

Sevastopol

BLACK SEA

CASPIAN SEA

38

The purges

After Stalin took power in the Soviet Union in 1927, he was terrified that his enemies would try to kill him. In 1934 a communist leader called Kirov was assassinated in Leningrad (actually on Stalin's orders, though no one knew this then). Stalin took the opportunity to have even more people arrested. They were put on trial and made to confess to huge crimes that they could not possibly have committed. Then they were sent to the *gulags* (concentration camps). These arrests were called *purges*.

Still Stalin did not feel safe. In 1937 he turned on the army. Thousands of officers were arrested and shot. Even the highest ranks were not safe. By 1939, the Red Army had lost half its officers, including three of its top five generals.

Most of the news about the purges was kept secret – as far as you can keep secret the arrest of millions of people, and the use of them as slave labour. But some people outside the Soviet Union knew very well what was going on. The Germans were particularly interested.

The Winter War

In December 1939 Stalin attacked Finland. It was the first proper war the Russians had fought since the purges, and they made a complete mess of it. The Finns beat them back easily, and it took months of fighting before the Russians forced the Finns to give in.

- Why do you think the Germans watched the events of the Winter War closely?

Hitler and the Soviet Union

Hitler hated the Russians.
- He thought Russians were 'sub-human'.
- There was a huge Jewish population in the Soviet Union, and Hitler hated Russian Jews even more than he hated other Russians.
- Hitler hated communism, and the Soviet Union was the only communist country in the world.
- The Soviet Union had vast areas of good farming land. This was the land Hitler wanted for the German people's *Lebensraum* (living space).

Source A
A German anti-Bolshevik poster.

Hitler made no secret of his feelings. The only real puzzle is why Stalin did not realise how Hitler felt.

Source B
Hitler set out his views on the Soviet Union many years before the war.

'When we speak of new land (for Germany) in Europe today we must principally bear in mind Russia and the border states subject to her.'
Adolf Hitler, *Mein Kampf*, 1924

Operation Barbarossa: 22 June 1941

The German attack was planned for June 1941. It was code-named *Barbarossa* ('Redbeard') after a German medieval hero.

The Russians were taken completely by surprise. The Germans destroyed the Russian air force on the ground, and smashed through the Russian defences. Surrounded and confused, over 600,000 Russian troops surrendered in the first week.

The Russians destroyed crops, bridges and railway lines in the Germans' path to stop them using them. They even managed to move over 1,000 factories and workshops out of danger and set them up hundreds of miles to the east. Even so, by November 1941 the Germans were just outside Moscow. On the Russian Front neither side showed the other any mercy, and it became a struggle to the death. It seemed that nothing could save the Soviet Union from total defeat.

Source C ▲

Russian peasants try to save belongings as their village burns.

◄ Source D

German troops in Rostov, 1941.

Clearing the land

The Nazis planned to clear the land they took in the Soviet Union to make room for German settlers, and that meant getting rid of the Russians who lived there. As the Germans tore into the Soviet Union, special army units called *Einsatzgruppen* followed them and began destroying whole villages and either murdering the people or sending them to slave labour camps.

40

Source E

A public hanging in occupied Russia. The Germans did not hesitate to execute anyone who opposed them in the Soviet Union.

Source F

Himmler, the head of the SS, gives instructions to his generals.

'Whether 10,000 Russian females fall down from exhaustion while digging an anti-tank ditch or not interests me only in so far as the anti-tank ditch for Germany is finished.'

1941

Some people, ruled by Stalin, welcomed the Germans. Non-Russians, like Latvians, Lithuanians, Ukrainians and Cossacks, decided that helping the Germans was the best way to win their independence.

Russian guerrilla fighters called *partisans* fought back against the Germans by burning crops, attacking German patrols or blowing up bridges or ammunition dumps. Like the Germans, they had no mercy on their enemies, and they expected none if they were caught.

Source G

Two young Ukrainian women partisans.

41

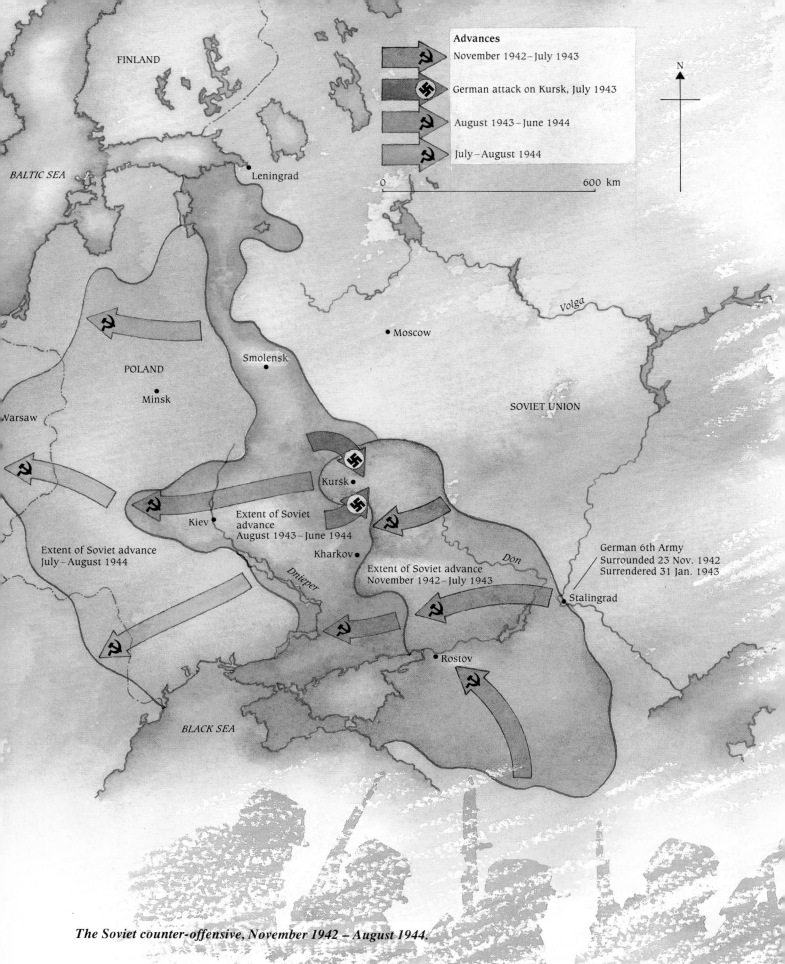

The Soviet counter-offensive, November 1942 – August 1944.

The Russians strike back

In December 1941 the Germans were just outside Moscow. The Muscovites dug anti-tank ditches and put up barricades. Stalin had his bags packed, ready to flee the city. Then he got some welcome news from Richard Sorge, his secret agent in Tokyo.

Stalin was holding some of his best troops back in reserve in case the Japanese attacked the Soviet Union in the east. The message from Tokyo said that the Japanese were planning to attack the United States, not the Soviet Union. Stalin stayed in Moscow, and launched his reserves against the Germans.

The Germans did not know what had hit them. They were forced back. As winter set in, their vehicles got stuck in deep mud and their weapons froze up and could not be fired. Moscow was saved.

Source H

German soldiers entrenched, *a painting by Franz Eichorst, a German artist.*

● *Why do you think Nazi censors would not allow this picture to be shown to the German public?*

But in the north, it was the Russians who were freezing. The Germans held the city of Leningrad, now known by its old name St Petersburg, in the grip of the worst siege in history.

The siege of Leningrad

The Germans cut Leningrad off from the rest of Russia and rained shells on it. Leningrad's beautiful palaces and churches were flattened. During the terrible winter of 1941, over 3,000 people starved to death *each day*. There were so many dead that they had to be buried in mass graves. Those left alive took to catching rats or crows to eat; then they began eating anything they could find, even Vaseline, sawdust, wallpaper paste and carpenter's glue.

The siege of Leningrad lasted 900 days and nearly one million Leningraders died in that time.

Stalingrad

When the weather got better in 1942 the Germans hit back. They had a new plan to seize Russia's oil fields.

The Germans caught the Russians by surprise and advanced very rapidly. Then the German commander, General von Paulus, decided to capture the city of Stalingrad.

The Russians in Stalingrad fought fiercely for every building and every street. The whole city was reduced to rubble, but still the Russians would not give in. Von Paulus wanted to pull his men out – but Hitler absolutely refused to allow it.

Russian reinforcements arrived and surrounded the Germans just as the terrible Russian winter was setting in. The Germans still did not have proper winter clothing, and they were running out of food and ammunition. They carried on fighting until January 1943, when von Paulus agreed to surrender. The Russians took nearly 90,000 Germans prisoner. This was a great turning point in the war. After Stalingrad the tide began to turn against Hitler.

Source J

The terrible siege of Leningrad. This couple are dragging their dead child to burial.

Source K

A Russian poster proclaiming the slogan 'For Stalin, For the Motherland' which united the Russian people.

44

Source L

Hitler's last message to von Paulus, in January 1943, reads as follows:

'Capitulation (surrender) is impossible. The 6th Army will do its historic duty at Stalingrad until the last man, in order to make possible the reconstruction of the Eastern Front.'

1 Why was the Soviet Union's Red Army so weak by 1941?

2 After the war, some people said that Hitler was not really to blame for the terrible things the Germans did. What evidence is there that Hitler was *personally* responsible for
◆ the terrible conditions in Leningrad
◆ the disaster at Stalingrad?

3 Why do you think the Germans failed to conquer the whole of the Soviet Union? Explain your answer.

4 Explain why the fighting in Russia was so bitter and vicious.

1941: Japanese attack Pearl Harbor

Without any warning, on 7 December Japanese planes bombed the American fleet at Pearl Harbor in Hawaii, and attacked British positions in Malaya. The Allies were taken completely by surprise, and the American fleet was badly damaged in the attack on Pearl Harbor.

1941: Japanese aircraft sink HMS Prince of Wales *and* Repulse

The British sent HMS *Prince of Wales* and HMS *Repulse* as a 'vague menace' to warn the Japanese not to attack the British base at Singapore. Without air cover the ships were defenceless when Japanese torpedo bombers found them and they were quickly sunk, taking hundreds of men to their deaths.

1942: Singapore surrenders to the Japanese

The Japanese swept through the British colonies in Asia, taking Hong Kong and Malaya. In February 1942 they took the mighty British fortress of Singapore. Singapore's heavy guns faced out to sea, but the Japanese attacked from the land. When the city's water supply ran out, the British commander had to surrender.

1942: Philippines fall to Japanese

General Douglas MacArthur led a fierce American defence of the Philippines, but the Japanese trapped the Americans in the narrow Bataan peninsula and forced them to surrender. As MacArthur left, he vowed 'I shall return'. As many as 10,000 Americans died in a terrible 'death march' from Bataan to prison camps in the north of the islands.

1942: Battle of Midway

The Japanese were steaming towards Midway Island in the middle of the Pacific when the Americans intercepted them. The battle was fought almost entirely by aircraft from aircraft carriers – the two fleets never saw each other. The Americans sank five Japanese carriers and lost one of their own. The Japanese were forced back in confusion.

1943: Americans retake Guadalcanal

After Midway, the Americans began the long, slow process of attacking Japanese-held islands in the Pacific. It was known as 'island hopping'. They began with Guadalcanal in the Solomon Islands, where the Japanese kept up fanatical resistance for six months before finally giving in.

1943–44: British fight back in Burma

Specially trained British groups called Chindits fought behind Japanese lines in the jungles of Burma. In 1944 the Japanese tried to invade India with a contingent of anti-British Indian troops, but they were thrown back after a battle at Imphal. In China the American General 'Vinegar Joe' Stilwell helped the Chinese guerrillas operating against the Japanese. Very slowly, the Japanese were pushed back through the jungle.

1942–45: Americans bomb Japan

In 1942 General James Doolittle led a surprise bombing attack on Tokyo. The Americans continued heavy bombing of Japanese cities, killing thousands in terrible firestorms. Finally, in 1945 they dropped atom bombs on Hiroshima and Nagasaki, devastating both cities.

8 Pearl Harbor

On 7 December 1941, Japanese planes attacked the American Pacific Fleet at Pearl Harbor. This brought the USA into the war.

Why did Japan decide to go to war with the strongest country in the world?

Understanding Japan

Japan in the 1930s seemed at first sight like any other modern country; but much of the country's old way of life survived. The Japanese still regarded their Emperor as a god. Many young Japanese officers were ready to fight and even die for their Emperor, like the samurai warriors of old. All they needed was a war.

Vladivostok

Sea of Japan

JAPAN

Peking

KOREA

Hiroshima

Tokyo

Nagasaki

Yellow Sea

OKINAWA

CHINA

Assam

IWO JI

INDIA

FORMOSA

Hong Kong

BURMA

Manila

Rangoon

Bay of Bengal

SIAM

Philippines

GU

Bangkok

Ceylon

South China Sea

Indian Ocean

Malaya

Singapore

Borneo

Celebes

Sumatra

DUTCH EAST INDIES

Timor Sea

Java

Timor

Darwin

Furthest Japanese
advance by July 1942

American advance

American air
attacks on Japan

British advances

The war in the Far East.

48

AUSTRAL

Japan had many problems.

- **Raw materials** Japan depended almost entirely on other countries for the raw materials needed for its industries.
- **Population** The country of Japan is a small group of islands, but the population was growing at an alarming rate. Vast numbers of Japanese people went to live in America. In 1924 the Americans began to limit the numbers of Japanese allowed in.

The 'solution'

In the late 1920s Japan's army leaders saw one simple solution to these problems: Japan should set up its own empire, just as the Europeans had done. This would bring in raw materials and provide somewhere for the country's huge population to live.

The army and the navy began to take control of the government. Politicians who protested were murdered. By 1931, Japan's leaders felt ready to begin their conquests.

The Japanese plan to build up an empire began in China. The Chinese were already fighting a bitter civil war, but they settled their differences for the moment in order to fight the Japanese. The Japanese found themselves bogged down in a long guerrilla war. Then, in 1941, the Americans cut off their exports of oil to Japan. Without oil, the Japanese could not keep their troops in China.

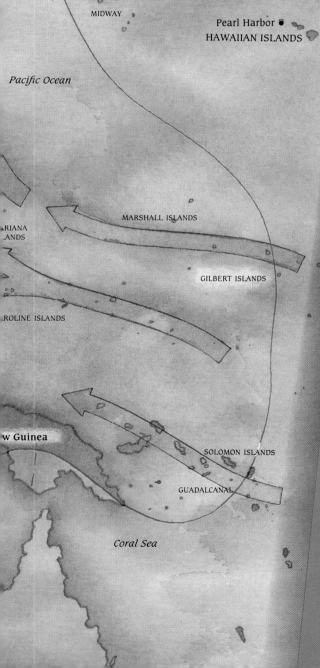

IMPERIAL JAPANESE GOVERNMENT

TOP SECRET

SUBJECT: Oil crisis

BACKGROUND

1. There is no sign of an end to the war in China. Our troops control all the important towns, but cannot control the countryside.

2. The Europeans and Americans demand that we should pull out of China. The Americans have now cut off oil exports. Without oil, our armies will have to pull out of China, and Japan will look weak and foolish.

THE PROBLEM

3. We must get hold of oil. There is plenty of oil in South East Asia. These areas, however, belong to the French, British and Dutch.

4. The French, British and Dutch are very weak. France and The Netherlands have been conquered by the Germans; the British are far too busy fighting the Germans in North Africa and Europe to defend their bases at Singapore and Hong Kong successfully. However, the United States is not at war, and will try to stop any move made by Japan to expand.

ACTION TO TAKE

5. We must have oil. Therefore we must conquer the British, Dutch and French possessions in South East Asia. They will not be able to fight back. We must find a way of crippling the Americans early on, before they have a chance to prepare. This means we must make a surprise attack.

The plan

Admiral Yamamoto came up with a plan to cripple the Americans. He discovered that on Sunday 7 December 1941 the whole American Pacific Fleet would be at anchor at Pearl Harbor in Hawaii. If the Japanese could destroy it, the Americans would be powerless to stop them taking over the Pacific and getting all the oil they wanted.

Source A

Pearl Harbor, 8.40 am, 7 December 1941.
The American fleet is destroyed by Japanese aircraft.

The attack

On the morning of 7 December, Japanese planes began bombing Pearl Harbor.

The Americans were stunned. There had been no warning, and they could do nothing to fight back. Five battleships and fourteen other vessels were sunk. The American aircraft were all neatly grouped together, and were easily destroyed by the Japanese bombs. The Japanese flew back to their aircraft carriers in triumph.

But was it a triumph? The ships sank in shallow water, and three of the battleships were repaired and set sail later in the war. Above all, the American aircraft carriers were not at Pearl Harbor on 7 December. Japan had started war with the United States, and would have to face the consequences.

Source B

Soon after the attack on Pearl Harbor, Admiral Yamamoto said:

'I fear we have only awakened a sleeping giant, and his reaction will be terrible.'

December 1941

Source C

Much later, historian A.J.P. Taylor wrote in 1961:

'The Japanese … never imagined they could penetrate to the New World and invade the United States. They did not even imagine that, if there were a prolonged war between them and the United States, they would win it. What they hoped for was that the United States, mainly involved in the European war, with so much of its resources directed towards Europe, would weary and would, in the end, come to a compromise with Japan.'

1 Explain in your own words why the Japanese decided to build up an empire.

2 Put yourself in the position of the Japanese leader Admiral Yamamoto, just before Pearl Harbor. Write a top-secret letter to Emperor Hirohito explaining why you have decided to launch a surprise attack on the USA.

9 The Holocaust

Of all the many atrocities in the Second World War, none was more horrifying than the Holocaust: the Nazis' attempt to exterminate the entire Jewish race.

Why did the Nazis commit this appalling crime?

Anti-Semitism, as hatred of Jewish people is called, had been common in Europe for many centuries. There had been massacres of Jewish communities in several European countries since the Middle Ages.

The Nazis were violently racist. From his earliest days, Hitler loathed Jewish people. He even thought that the defeat of Germany in the First World War and the communist revolution in Russia were part of a Jewish plot to take over the world.

Source A

In one of his earliest speeches Hitler blamed the Jews for the problems of the world.

'Already the Jews have destroyed Russia and now they turn on Germany. Out of envy the Jews want to destroy the spirit of Germany.'

Hitler, July 1922

Once in power the Nazis turned on the Jews of Germany. In 1933 Jews were banned from doing a number of well-paid jobs. Jews could not be German citizens and Jews were not allowed to marry other Germans. Nazi stormtroopers beat up Jews in the street, and a special newspaper printed anti-Jewish propaganda. Although they were the victims of violence and abuse, the destruction of the Jews was not an overnight event. In November 1938 there was a sign of even worse things to come when, in one night, synagogues were burned down all over Germany and many hundreds of Jews were murdered. Thousands of Jewish shops and homes were attacked; there was so much broken glass that the night became known as 'Kristallnacht' – the Night of Broken Glass. The Nazis even made their Jewish victims clear up the glass.

Source B

A Jewish store daubed with Nazi graffiti, Berlin, 1933.

Source C

Paris, 1940, a Jewish man wearing a yellow star. In Germany and all occupied countries the Nazis forced Jewish people to wear yellow stars.

Source D

In May 1943, after four weeks of heroic resistance, the Jewish uprising in the Warsaw ghetto was finally crushed. What little remained of the ghetto was razed to the ground. Here a Jewish boy is being taken away to a concentration camp.

The extermination of the Jews began after the outbreak of the war. As German tanks rolled east, many Jews were captured in Poland, in the Ukraine and in the Soviet Union. Often whole villages of Jewish people were rounded up and massacred.

Ghettos

Those Jews who survived the initial German conquest were forced to move to special sealed-off areas in towns, called *ghettos*. The ghettos were run by special Jewish councils, who arranged for food to be distributed and for the children to go to school. But the ghettos were not safe: the Gestapo, Nazi police, and the SS, raided them regularly, to round people up and take them to their death.

Sometimes the Jews fought back. When in May 1943 the SS moved into the Warsaw ghetto in Poland, to their surprise the Jews fought back fiercely with guns they had managed to smuggle in. The SS brought up tanks and flame-throwers, but still the Jews kept on fighting. The SS were amazed, but in the end they crushed the resistance and sent the last inhabitants of the ghetto to death camps.

Source E

An inhabitant of the Warsaw ghetto gave this eye-witness account:

'We were happy and laughing. When we threw our grenades and saw German blood on the streets of Warsaw, which had been flooded with so much Jewish blood and tears, a great joy possessed us.'

Zivia Lubetkin

Source F

'Amazing! These bandits (Jews) would often rather stay inside burning buildings than be captured by us. And I have seen several leap, on fire, from blazing buildings and thus meet their death. Extraordinary!'

SS Major General Jürgen Stroop, April 1943

Source G

An eye-witness gave this account of a mass execution of Jews in a forest in Poland.

'Without screaming or weeping these people undressed … (A) father was holding the hand of a boy about 10 years old and speaking to him softly; the boy was fighting his tears.

(Nearby there was) a tremendous grave. People were wedged closely together and lying on top of each other so that only their heads were visible. Nearly all had blood running over their shoulders from their heads. … I estimated that it contained about a thousand people. I looked for the man who did the shooting. He was an SS man, who sat at the edge of the narrow end of the pit, his feet dangling into the pit. He had a tommy gun on his knees and was smoking a cigarette.'

Quoted in William Shirer, *The Rise and Fall of the Third Reich*, 1973

The location of concentration camps in Germany and the occupied countries.

The Wannsee Conference and 'the Final Solution'

In January 1942 a group of leading Nazis met at the smart Berlin suburb of Wannsee to decide on a cheap, efficient way of exterminating the Jews of Europe. This Wannsee Conference drew up one of the most frightful plans ever hatched: they decided to wipe out the entire Jewish population using poison gas.

Some of the concentration camps would be converted into special *extermination camps* to carry out 'the Final Solution' to what the Nazis called 'the Jewish Problem'.

Within a few weeks the first extermination camp was ready. It was near the Polish town of Oswiecim. The Germans called it Auschwitz.

● Why do you think the Nazis called the plan to exterminate the Jewish race 'the Final Solution'?

Auschwitz

Auschwitz was vast, covering 47 square kilometres (18 square miles). It had a chemicals factory, with a large slave labour camp attached. In 1942 Auschwitz became an extermination camp.

Jews, Gypsies, homosexuals and prisoners of all kinds were sent to Auschwitz from all over Europe. They travelled in cattle trucks, often standing up all the way, with no food or water. Many died on the journey.

When they arrived at Auschwitz, they were immediately sorted into those who could work and those who could not. People who could work were taken away; people who were too old or too ill to work, as well as most of the children, were all sent straight to the gas chambers. Usually, to prevent panic the victims were told they were going to have a shower, and sometimes music played as they went in. At some camps, prisoners were used by SS doctors for scientific experiments.

Source I

Ovens used to burn the bodies of the dead in Belsen concentration camp.

Source H

A French prisoner described how people were gassed at Auschwitz.

'The men stood on one side, the women on the other. They were addressed in a very polite and friendly way: "You have been on a journey. You are dirty. You will take a bath. Get undressed quickly." Towels and soap were handed out, and then suddenly the brutes woke up and showed their true faces: this horde of people, these men and women were driven outside with hard blows and forced both summer and winter to go the few hundred metres to the "Shower Room". … The doors were shut … then SS Unterscharführer Moll threw the gas in through a little vent. One could hear fearful screams, but a few moments later there was complete silence.

Twenty to twenty-five minutes later, the doors and windows were opened to ventilate the rooms and the corpses were thrown at once into pits to be burnt. But beforehand the dentists had searched every mouth to pull out the gold teeth. The women were also searched to see if they had not hidden jewellery in the intimate parts of their bodies, and their hair was cut off and methodically placed in sacks for industrial purposes.'

Source J

Auschwitz. Most people arrived here by train, in cattle trucks.

Source K

'As many as twenty-five persons were put at one time into a specially constructed van in which pressure could be increased or decreased as required. The purpose was to find out the effects of high altitude and of rapid parachute descents on human beings. Most of the prisoners who were made use of died as a result of these experiments, from internal haemorrhages of the lungs or the brain.'

Records of the Nuremberg War Trials, 1946

Source L

Fritz Stangl, Commandant of Treblinka, another extermination camp, explains how he felt about his victims.

'**Q**: Would it be true to say that you finally felt the Jews weren't human beings?

A: Cargo. They were cargo. … I remember … the pits full of blue-black corpses. It had nothing to do with humanity – it couldn't have; a mass of rotting flesh. Wirth (a senior SS official) said, "What shall we do with this garbage?" I think that started me thinking of them as cargo.'

1971

Source M

A mass grave for the victims of the Holocaust.

After the war, many Nazis were tried and executed for their part in the Holocaust. Adolf Eichmann was one of the most well-known Nazi war criminals. He helped work out the details of 'the Final Solution', and was present at the Wannsee Conference. From then till the end of the war, it was his job to organise for Jews, especially in Hungary, to be sent to the extermination camps.

After the war he was captured by the Americans but escaped to South America under a false name. In 1960 he was kidnapped by the Israelis and put on trial in Jerusalem. He was hanged in 1962.

Source N

Eichmann told his Israeli interrogator:

'I'm covered with guilt, Herr Hauptmann (Captain), I know that. But I had nothing to do with killing Jews. I've never killed a Jew. And I've never ordered anyone to kill a Jew.'

Jochen von Lang, *Eichmann Interrogated*, 1983

Source O

Adolf Eichmann on trial in Jerusalem.

- It is true that Eichmann never personally murdered anyone. Look back at the events for which he was actually responsible. Was he right when he said
  - he had never killed a Jew
  - he had never ordered anyone to kill a Jew?

PORTRAIT OF A NAZI:

ADOLF EICHMANN

EARLY YEARS He came from a large family in Austria. His parents were regular church-goers. Eichmann went to the same secondary school as Hitler. He did not work hard and was taken out of school by his father, who sent him to technical college.

WORK He was an apprentice in an Austrian electrical company for a couple of years, before getting a job as a travelling salesman. In 1933, during the worldwide slump, he was made redundant and went to Germany to look for work.

NAZI PARTY Eichmann joined the Nazi Party and the SS part-time in 1932. When he went to Germany in 1933 he became a full-time member of the SS. He quickly won promotion and became a Lieutenant Colonel.

1 Using information in this unit, construct a time-line showing what the Nazis said and did about Jewish people in the period 1922–45.

2 What evidence is there in this unit to show that some Germans did not consider the Jews to be human beings?

3 Why do you think the Nazis treated the Jews in such an appalling way?

4 Suppose you were the Israeli prosecutor in 1962. What charges could you bring against Eichmann? (*Note*: You must be able to prove the charges.)

10 Bombing

In 1992 a statue of Sir Arthur Harris, the commander of RAF Bomber Command, was unveiled in London. Many people protested, saying that the bombing of civilian targets in Germany was little more than murder. Others said it was vital in winning the war.

What did bombing actually achieve?

Bombing had to be carefully planned. Targets tended to be of four types.

- **Military sites**
  The German Luftwaffe bombed British radar stations and airfields during the Battle of Britain. The RAF bombed the German forces gathering in France to invade Britain, and U-boat bases during the Battle of the Atlantic.

- **Communications**
  Roads, railways and bridges, which the enemy needed in order to move troops, were targets for the bombing.

- **Industry**
  Modern armies need vast stocks of weapons and ammunition. Both sides viewed the factories that provided these supplies as *legitimate* bombing targets.

- **Civilians**
  At the start of the war, each side tried to avoid hitting areas where ordinary people lived, but bombs often missed factories or bridges and hit houses instead. The Germans launched the *Blitz* on British cities; later the Allies bombed German cities even more ferociously.

Getting to the target was difficult because of enemy fighter aircraft and anti-aircraft fire, called *flak*. The only sure defence was to have fighters to escort the bombers, but fighters could only carry enough fuel to fly fairly short distances, so most groups of bombers had to travel on to their targets alone.

Source A

A little girl is rescued from a bombed building in London.

The Germans bomb Britain

The first heavy bombing began in 1940 during the Battle of Britain. London, Coventry and other British cities were heavily bombed by the Luftwaffe in what was called the Blitz. In Plymouth, the bombing was so fierce that the people nearly rioted, but for the most part bombing merely strengthened people's resolve to fight on.

The big raids on Germany continue. British war plants share with the R.A.F. credit for these giant operations.

THE ATTACK BEGINS IN THE FACTORY

Source D

This poster showing Lancaster bombers attacking a target in Germany gives a vivid picture of a night-time bombing raid. What was the purpose of this poster?

A formation of US B17 bombers on a daylight bombing raid.

Source F

A stricken B17 Flying Fortress over Berlin on a daylight raid. Its tailplane has been mangled by bombs from aircraft higher in the formation. Losses like this happened because bomber formations often contained hundreds of aircraft.

The Allies bomb Germany

The RAF began bombing Germany as soon as the Germans bombed London, and went on bombing until the end of the war. For most of the war, bombing was the only way the British had of actually hitting back at Germany. The bombers aimed mostly at German industrial towns and U-boat bases. Germany was too far away for British fighters to escort the bombers, so the Germans were able to shoot down hundreds of aircraft. Those that did get through often missed their targets. In 1941 more British aircrew were killed than German civilians.

After 1941, the Americans took over bombing in daylight, and the RAF switched to bombing at night. It cost the Americans hundreds of aircraft, but it also meant the Allies could launch massive raids on German cities. A single raid by a thousand bombers destroyed the city of Cologne, and in 1943 the centre of Hamburg was destroyed in four nights of heavy bombing that created a terrible *firestorm*.

The devastated centre of Dresden.

Dresden

It is estimated that in February 1945 more than 35,000 people were killed in a massive British bombing raid that destroyed the city of Dresden in eastern Germany. Dresden was a particularly beautiful city, with no heavy industry. In February 1945 it was packed with refugees fleeing from the Russians.

There have been many arguments about the Dresden raid.

Was it justified?

1 The Russians wanted a heavy bombing raid on a city to destroy bridges and railway lines. It would also clog up the roads with refugees so that the Germans would not be able to move their troops.

2 The British government Target Committee considered the Russian request, and decided Dresden should be the target. They told Bomber Command to arrange the raid.

3 Dresden was quite unprepared for the raid. The whole of the centre of the city was destroyed, partly by bombs and partly by a massive firestorm.

How a firestorm works

Experienced 'pathfinders' lead the attack with incendiary bombs to guide the main attack.

Bombers drop mixture of incendiary and high explosive bombs.

Allies bomb in waves. The second wave strikes as the clearing up is in progress after the first raid.

Burning debris

Updraft of air spreads burning debris, creating further fires, and creates vacuum at the centre.

VACUUM

Small incendiaries lodge in roofs and start fires.

Wooden buildings burn easily.

High explosive bombs shatter walls and windows, letting in air which feeds fire.

Heat at centre is intense enough to incinerate people instantly.

Debris blocks streets and prevents fire services getting through.

Tarmac melts, frying people alive.

Large incendiaries penetrate buildings and start fires inside.

Vacuum sucks air out of cellars, replacing it with poisonous carbon monoxide.

The vacuum created by the updraft of air sucks in air to fill it, creating hurricane-speed winds strong enough to uproot trees and suck people into the centre of the firestorm.

Source I

When Churchill began to doubt whether the raid was justified, Harris wrote to him.

Dear Prime Minister

The Dresden Raid

What really makes any sort of (German) recovery almost impossible is ... the complete dislocation of transportation ... You will remember that Dresden was recommended by the Target Committee as a transportation target as well as on other grounds... Attacks on cities ... are strategically justified in so far as they tend to shorten the war and so preserve the lives of Allied soldiers ... I do not personally regard the whole of the remaining cities of Germany as worth the bones of one British Grenadier.

Yours sincerely

Arthur Harris

RAF Bomber Command

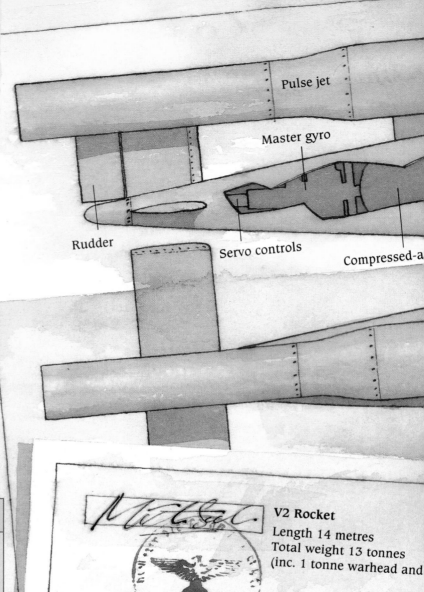

Pulse jet

Master gyro

Rudder

Servo controls

Compressed-a

Source J — German war production

	1940	1942	1944
Military aircraft	10,200	14,200	39,500
Tanks	1,600	6,300	19,000
Heavy guns	4,400	5,100	24,900

Adapted from Max Hastings, *Bomber Command*, 1979

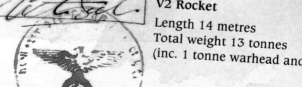

V2 Rocket

Length 14 metres
Total weight 13 tonnes
(inc. 1 tonne warhead and

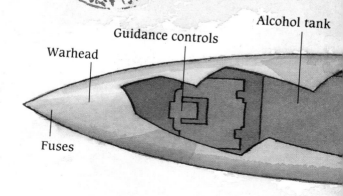

Alcohol tank

Guidance controls

Warhead

Fuses

Source K

Arthur Harris planning the bombing offensive against Germany.

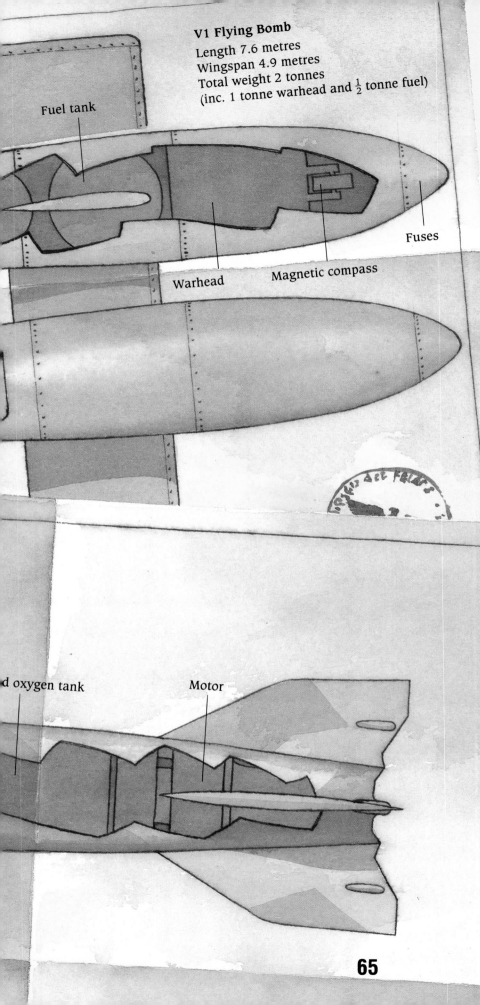

V1 Flying Bomb
Length 7.6 metres
Wingspan 4.9 metres
Total weight 2 tonnes
(inc. 1 tonne warhead and $\frac{1}{2}$ tonne fuel)

Fuel tank

Fuses

Warhead   Magnetic compass

d oxygen tank   Motor

Source L

A leading Nazi later commented on the impact of bombing.

'We would have been able to keep our promise of delivering forty boats a month by early in 1945, however badly the war was going otherwise, if air raids had not destroyed a third of the submarines at the dockyards.'

Albert Speer speaking in the 1960s, quoted in D. Saward, *Bomber Harris*, 1984

New terror weapons

Towards the end of the war the Germans began to use two new weapons: the V1, a small pilotless aircraft packed with explosive – a flying bomb; and the V2, a giant rocket with an explosive warhead. V stood for *Vergeltung*, retaliation, because British and American bombers had devastated German cities. These weapons did damage London but no worse than the raids during 1940–41.

Hitler's scientists were on the point of discovering how to split the atom and might have developed an atom bomb if Germany had not been defeated in 1945.

A television company has decided to stage a debate on whether the British bombing of German cities was justified. Using the information from this unit, produce a report that can be used in the televised debate, either for or against the bombing. You may wish to mention

◆ the different types of target
◆ civilian casualties
◆ civilian morale
◆ German attacks on British cities
◆ German war production.

Many important strategic decisions had to be taken during the war, and the Allied leaders met up at a series of conferences.

Meeting 1, in Newfoundland, Canada: The Atlantic Charter

In 1941 Churchill crossed the Atlantic on HMS *Prince of Wales* to meet the President of the still-neutral United States, Franklin D. Roosevelt.

Welcome aboard, Mr President. I wish I could welcome you into the war with Germany too.

Not a chance, Winston: the American people aren't ready for that yet. But I'll give you what help I can.

This is not just a war between Britain and Germany…

…it's being fought to defend freedom in the whole world, and to stop anyone invading other countries.

They agreed to sign the *Atlantic Charter*, to say what the war was about.

The Charter was a clear warning to Germany that the USA would not stay neutral for long.

Meeting 2, in Persia (Iran): Tehran, 1943

The Russian people are dying in their millions! Why will you not open a Second Front against the Hitlerites?

But the Germans have you pinned down in Italy, and they don't need many men to do it. What I want is a full-scale invasion of Europe!

We have: we've invaded Italy.

And we've agreed to launch a Second Front in France next year.

By 1943, Britain, the Soviet Union and the USA were all at war with Germany. Stalin was desperate for the western Allies to launch a *Second Front* to relieve the German pressure on the Russian Front. He thought the other leaders were just wasting time. It was time they all met.

The Allies agreed that the Soviet Union could keep the lands it had taken in the Baltic, and that German leaders would be put on trial for war crimes after the war. Churchill and Roosevelt also agreed to invade Europe, to take the pressure off the Russians.

CONFERENCES

Meeting 3, in the Soviet Union: Yalta, 1945

We agree to divide Germany and Austria between us, and I want all Russians taken in German uniform handed over. I also want to keep all the land I've taken in Poland.

He can't have that. We declared war in the first place to protect Poland.

Now, Winston, none of your old Russia-bashing.

It won't be difficult to get around free elections - not if I have my troops at the polling stations.

Why can't Roosevelt see? Stalin is as dangerous as Hitler was. It's appeasement all over again!

I haven't fought this terrible war just to restore the British Empire.

By the start of 1945, the Germans were retreating everywhere. Victory for the Allies was only a matter of time. But what would they do after the war? They met at Yalta, in the Soviet Union, to decide.

Churchill tried to warn Roosevelt of the dangers of giving the Russians too much. But Roosevelt trusted Stalin more than he trusted Churchill. And Stalin promised there would be free elections in eastern Europe, including Poland.

Meeting 4, in Germany: Potsdam, 1945

After Germany surrendered, the Allies met up again, this time at Potsdam, just outside Berlin. This time there were some new faces. The British elected a new Prime Minister, Clement Attlee, to replace Churchill. In America, Roosevelt had died. The new President, Harry S Truman, was more suspicious of the Russians.

You ought to know, Marshal, that the US possesses a weapon – a bomb – more powerful than any weapon in the world.

Good. I hope you use it soon – against the Japanese.

Marshal Stalin, if you think you can keep your troops all over eastern Europe, forget it!

Welcome, Mr President.

Potsdam ended in deadlock. Stalin refused to remove his troops from Europe. All the Allies could agree on was to put the Nazi leaders on trial at Nuremberg. Truman thought it was time to let Stalin into a secret.

Truman did use the bomb on Japan, but he was also warning Stalin. Already, a new war seemed to be brewing.

11 D-Day

For three years, most of the fighting against Germany was going on in Russia. Many people began to ask when the British and Americans would open a second front against the Nazis.

Why did it take so long to open the Second Front?

Hitler had built a huge line of defences all along the Atlantic coast, from Denmark to Spain. He called it his Atlantic Wall. The Allies soon learned how strong it was.

In 1942 a large force of Canadian and British troops attacked the French port of Dieppe. The Germans were well prepared and cut the attackers to pieces.

In 1941 and 1942, the Russians did most of the fighting against the German army. They were desperate for the British to attack the Germans in the west, to relieve the pressure, but the British were unable to do this alone. They had to wait for American help.

In 1942 the British were still fighting a difficult battle against Field Marshal Rommel in North Africa. They wanted to finish this campaign before opening any new fronts.

Italy

Instead, Churchill suggested attacking Italy. He thought this would be much easier than an attack on the Germans in France. It turned out to be more difficult than he imagined. The Germans rushed troops into Italy and fought every inch of the way. The Americans and British were soon pinned down in the mountains and the advance seemed to come to a halt.

Planning

By 1944 Churchill was ready to agree to an attack on German-occupied France. The Allies practised on beaches in England. One practice ended in tragedy. As the Americans were coming ashore at Slapton Sands in Devon, two German boats attacked the landing crafts, and hundreds of Americans were drowned. If this had happened on the day of the real invasion it would have been a disaster.

Source A

General Dwight D. Eisenhower, centre, with his council of war. Montgomery is on his left.

Preparing for D-Day

The invasion was code-named *Operation Overlord*. The Supreme Commander for Overlord was the American General Dwight D. Eisenhower. His deputy was the British General Montgomery. The German commander in France was their old enemy from North Africa: Rommel.

Transporting a massive army across the Channel onto a defended beach was not easy, and careful, detailed planning went into Overlord.

1 Where should Eisenhower attack?

The Germans expected the Allies to attack near Calais, where the Channel is very narrow. The Allies bombed the area around Calais, to make the Germans think the attack was coming there. But in fact a surprise attack was planned further west, in Normandy.

2 What were the German defences like?

The Germans had put obstacles on the beaches to tear open the bottoms of any boats that attempted to land. The invasion would be at low tide, when the obstacles would be exposed on the shore.

3 How would the troops deal with the German heavy guns and tanks?

The Allies would be bringing their own tanks and heavy guns with them. Special amphibious tanks were designed which could float ashore, rather like the modern hovercraft. The tanks would lay a track along the beach for vehicles to move on.

4 How could the air force and navy help the invading army?

Before D-Day the Allies would bomb and destroy all the railways, bridges and roads in the invasion area, to stop the Germans bringing in reinforcements. Also, paratroops would land the night before the invasion and seize all the bridges and crossings that would be needed by the Allies. British minesweepers would clear a way for the invasion fleet. But the biggest question was still:

5 How could troops and supplies be landed safely?

British engineers invented floating harbours – *Mulberries* – which were towed across the Channel.

6 Wouldn't the Germans know the invasion was coming?

Yes, but they would not know *when*, nor exactly *where*. And if the bombing of Calais worked, the Germans would be ready and prepared – but in the wrong place. Nothing was left to chance. The invasion, code-named *D-Day*, was scheduled for early June 1944, but it proved very windy and stormy. The meteorologists forecast a slight break on 6 June. 'OK,' said Eisenhower, 'let's go.'

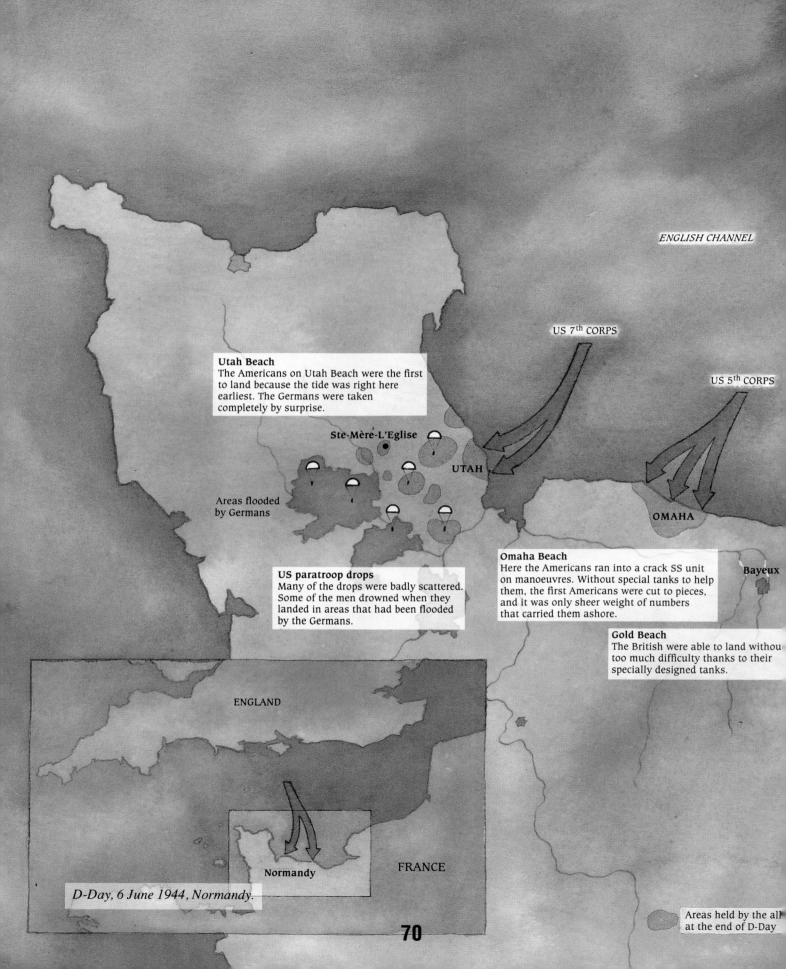

ENGLISH CHANNEL

US 7th CORPS

US 5th CORPS

Utah Beach
The Americans on Utah Beach were the first to land because the tide was right here earliest. The Germans were taken completely by surprise.

Ste-Mère-L'Eglise

UTAH

Areas flooded by Germans

OMAHA

Bayeux

US paratroop drops
Many of the drops were badly scattered. Some of the men drowned when they landed in areas that had been flooded by the Germans.

Omaha Beach
Here the Americans ran into a crack SS unit on manoeuvres. Without special tanks to help them, the first Americans were cut to pieces, and it was only sheer weight of numbers that carried them ashore.

Gold Beach
The British were able to land withou too much difficulty thanks to their specially designed tanks.

ENGLAND

Normandy

FRANCE

D-Day, 6 June 1944, Normandy.

Areas held by the all at the end of D-Day

70

TISH 30ᵗʰ CORPS

BRITISH + CANADIAN 1ˢᵗ CORPS

GOLD

JUNO

rromanches

SWORD

Caen

Sword Beach
The Germans launched a counter-attack
to cut off the British, but it was driven off.

British paratroop drops
The drops here went well
and the paratroops
captured most of their targets.

Juno Beach
The tide was coming in by the time the
Canadians landed, and many of their
landing craft were torn to pieces by
the German obstacles.

Falaise

71

The Germans were caught completely by surprise. They were still expecting the main attack to be near Calais, and they did not have many troops stationed in Normandy. Even after D-Day, they kept most of their troops near Calais, in case the main attack was still to come there. Now it seemed that nothing would stop the Allies. Winston Churchill and King George VI crossed the Channel to visit the beaches. General de Gaulle, leader of the Free French in exile, rushed over to get back on French soil again. In Normandy itself, people offered the Allied troops wine and danced in the streets as they advanced. But things were not over yet.

Mulberry

At first the Mulberry harbours worked very well, but on 17 June they were wrecked by a storm. The port of Cherbourg was so badly destroyed that when the allies captured it they had to carry on using the Mulberry harbours.

The bocage

The Normandy countryside is criss-crossed by tall, thick hedges, known in French as the *bocage*. The bocage provided excellent cover for the Germans, who fought for every hedge and field. It took the Allies weeks to break through this fierce German resistance.

Caen

The British launched a massive bombardment to force the Germans out of the city of Caen. The Germans surrendered, but Caen was completely destroyed.

The Falaise Gap

The Allies surrounded the Germans in an area around the town of Falaise that became known as the Falaise Gap, and bombed them mercilessly with fighter-bombers. Nearly 10,000 Germans were killed in one of the bloodiest battles of the war.

How the Mulberry Plan worked

A temporary sea wall of scuttled ships and concrete blocks provided shelter for the piers where the ships could dock. The piers stood on adjustable steel legs and were linked to the land by pontoon bridges.

Source C

Rocket-firing Typhoons at the Falaise Gap, Normandy,
1944 *by Frank Wootton*.

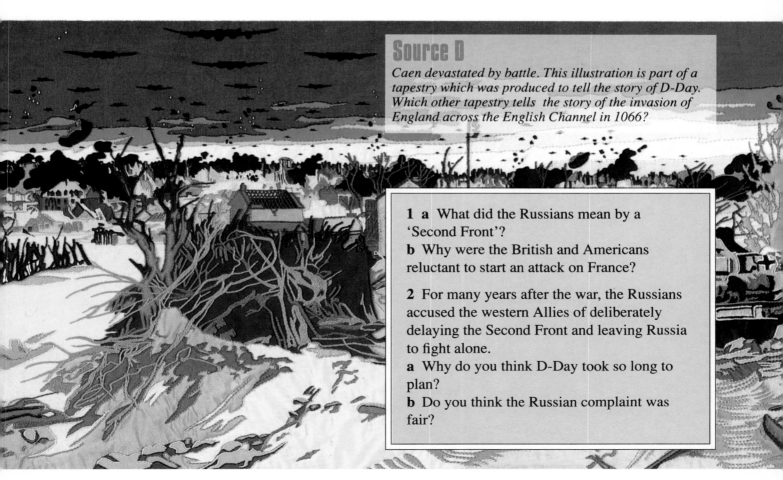

Source D

*Caen devastated by battle. This illustration is part of a
tapestry which was produced to tell the story of D-Day.
Which other tapestry tells the story of the invasion of
England across the English Channel in 1066?*

1 a What did the Russians mean by a
'Second Front'?
b Why were the British and Americans
reluctant to start an attack on France?

2 For many years after the war, the Russians
accused the western Allies of deliberately
delaying the Second Front and leaving Russia
to fight alone.
a Why do you think D-Day took so long to
plan?
b Do you think the Russian complaint was
fair?

12 Germany collapses

With the Russians advancing from the east and the British and Americans racing forwards in the west, Hitler was as determined as ever to fight on.

Why did the Germans not surrender sooner?

The Bomb Plot

Part of the answer to this question lies in what happened on 20 July 1944. On that day, Hitler held a conference with some of his generals. One officer, Count von Stauffenberg, was called away to the telephone and left the room, leaving his briefcase behind. The briefcase contained a bomb. No sooner was Stauffenberg out of the room than the bomb went off.

Hitler was incredibly lucky. The thick oak table in the room protected him from the blast, though the others in the room were badly injured and some were killed. But he was badly shaken, and determined to get his revenge.

It soon became clear that many German officers had known about the plot. The SS began to round them up. Colonels, generals, even field marshals were arrested and shot. Others were sentenced to death and immediately taken out to be strangled with piano wire and strung up on meat hooks.

Most of the army were terrified. To stop them surrendering to the Allies, Hitler threatened to shoot the family of any soldier who gave himself up.

In the east, the Germans were only too well aware of the terrible things they had done in Russia. They knew how they had treated Russian prisoners and they were afraid that if they surrendered the Russians would kill them.

The Battle of the Bulge

At Christmas 1944 Hitler launched a massive counter-attack against the Americans in France. The Americans were taken by surprise, and the Germans quickly cut them off. German soldiers disguised as Americans spread confusion behind the American lines. The Germans called on the Americans to surrender, but the American general in command replied, 'Nuts!'

The Germans could not keep up the attack for long. Their tanks ran out of fuel and the Americans were able to push them back. Hitler's last gamble had failed.

Source A
Hitler showing Mussolini the room where he survived the assassination attempt.

The fall of Berlin

Meanwhile, in the east the Russians under Marshal Zhukov were closing in on Berlin. On 25 April 1945, Russian and American troops met up at Torgau, only 120 kilometres from Berlin.

Hitler and his most trusted followers withdrew to a special underground bunker. There he carried on giving orders to a German army that no longer existed. He even took the opportunity to get married to a woman called Eva Braun, and allowed his followers to organise a dance, which was held in the canteen – while overhead Russian soldiers advanced through the streets of Berlin.

Finally, on 30 April 1945, Hitler and his new wife killed themselves. He shot himself through the mouth; Eva swallowed poison.

On 7 May Germany surrendered to the Allies. In Britain and America there was wild rejoicing and dancing in the streets to celebrate VE day – Victory in Europe – on 8 May 1945. People were delighted that finally the war was over.

But it wasn't. In Asia the war with Japan was still going on, and there was every sign that it was getting tougher. It was to be several months more before people in Britain could celebrate VJ day, Victory over Japan, on 15 August 1945.

Source C

A Russian soldier hoists the Soviet flag over the Reichstag building, with the ruins of Berlin in the background.

Source B

American Sherman tanks waiting to go into action in the Ardennes, December 1944.

---

1 Why do you think the German army fought particularly hard after the Bomb Plot went wrong?

2 What did the Battle of the Bulge show about the German army by the end of 1944?

3 Put the following explanations as to why the Germans did not surrender until 1945 into a rank order of importance.
◆ Hitler had lost touch with reality.
◆ The Germans were terrified of the Russians.
◆ The German army could still fight well.
◆ Hitler never allowed his generals to surrender.
◆ The German army was terrified of the SS.

Explain your choice.

13 The atom bomb

In August 1945 the Americans dropped atom bombs on Hiroshima and Nagasaki, and destroyed both cities. There have been furious arguments about this decision ever since.

Why did the Americans decide to drop the atom bombs?

The Manhattan Project

The Allies were terrified that the Germans might construct an atom bomb first. They bombed the German laboratories. The Germans had another problem too. They had forced many of the leading nuclear physicists to flee to Britain or the United States because they were Jewish. Without their help, the Germans could only work slowly, and they still had not made a breakthrough when Germany surrendered in May 1945.

In the United States, Roosevelt gathered together a group of American, Canadian and British scientists, led by an American, Robert Oppenheimer, to work on the atom bomb. It was code-named the *Manhattan Project*.

The scientists worked in secret in a remote village called Los Alamos, in the middle of the New Mexico desert.

In July 1945, the first atom bomb was ready. When the scientists tested it, it left an enormous crater many kilometres wide. The scientists were delighted that the bomb worked, but over-awed at its power. When the bomb went off, Oppenheimer quoted an old Indian poem: 'I am become Death, the destroyer of worlds'.

It was too late to use the bomb on Germany, but the war with Japan was still going on as fiercely as ever. Should the bomb be used there?

Source A

An atom bomb test explosion, New Mexico, 16 July 1945.

How to defeat Japan

Now that the war with Germany was over, people were impatient to win the war with Japan. But how?

There seemed to be five ways:

1 Invasion
The Japanese were putting up fanatical resistance on the Pacific islands and costing the Americans thousands of casualties. The Americans calculated that invading Japan would cost a million men.

2 Blockade
Japan had no raw materials of its own, and a tight blockade would be a disaster for that country.

3 Bombing
The Americans were bombing Japan heavily. In March 1945 a single raid on Tokyo killed 80,000 people. On the other hand, heavy bombing on its own had not forced either Britain or Germany to give in.

4 Russian help
So far, Stalin had kept out of the Japanese war, but now Germany was dealt with, he became interested in the east. The Russians could attack the Japanese in Manchuria and China. The Americans did not want the Russians to advance that far.

That left one last possibility.

5 Use the atom bomb
But was it right to use it? Even the scientists could not agree.

The man who had to make the decision was the new American President, Harry S Truman.

Dropping the bomb would definitely
- kill thousands of Japanese civilians
- give a terrible shock to the Japanese government and people.

Dropping the bomb might
- make the Japanese surrender quickly
- save thousands of Allied lives (because now the Allies would not have to invade Japan)
- stop the Russians from advancing too far.

Not dropping the bomb would probably
- mean that the Allies would have to invade Japan to force her to surrender.

Not dropping the bomb might
- make the war drag on for another year, with further heavy Allied casualties
- give the Russians a chance to advance into China, and possibly even share in the occupation of Japan after the war
- suggest that the Americans were afraid to use it.

Truman decided to use the bomb.

On 6 August 1945, a single US bomber dropped the first atom bomb, nicknamed 'Little Boy', over the Japanese city of Hiroshima. It exploded with a blinding flash. Hiroshima was completely destroyed.

Three days later a second bomber took off. It carried another atom bomb of a different design, nicknamed 'Fat Man'. The weather was cloudy, and the pilot could not find his target. He set off instead for his reserve target, the city of Nagasaki. This was where the first Americans had arrived in Japan a hundred years before. 'Fat Man' destroyed the city.

Source C

'Little Boy', the first atom bomb to be used as a weapon, had the power of 20,000 tons of TNT.

Source B

An Allied prisoner of war in Japan said after the war:

'There is no doubt in my mind that these atomic bombs saved many more lives than the tens of thousands that they killed. They saved the lives of tens of thousands of prisoners of war, of hundreds of thousands of Allied Servicemen and almost certainly of millions of Japanese – for, let there be no mistake, if the Emperor and his cabinet had decided to fight on, the Japanese would, literally, have fought to the last man.'

Fletcher-Cooke, *The Emperor's Guest*, 1971

Source D

Allied prisoners of war in a Japanese camp – a painting by Leslie Cole.

Source E

Mr Tanimoto was 3 kilometres away from the centre of the explosion in Hiroshima.

'A tremendous flash of light cut across the sky … Mr Tanimoto threw himself between two big rocks – he felt a sudden pressure and then splinters and pieces of board and fragments of tile fell on him. He heard no roar … Mr Tanimoto met hundreds and hundreds who were fleeing. The eyebrows of some were burned off and slime hung from their faces and hands. Some were vomiting as they walked.'

John Hersey, *Hiroshima*, 1946

Source F

The devastated city of Hiroshima, 6 August, 1945. Between 75,000 and 100,000 people died in the blast. Within five years nearly half a million people died from the radiation effects of the bombing of Hiroshima and Nagasaki.

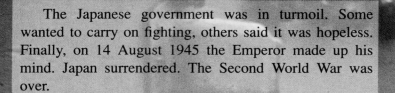

The Japanese government was in turmoil. Some wanted to carry on fighting, others said it was hopeless. Finally, on 14 August 1945 the Emperor made up his mind. Japan surrendered. The Second World War was over.

Source G

The official surrender of Japan, Tokyo Bay, 2 September 1945 on the quarterdeck of USS Missouri.

Source H

Akihiro Takahashi was at school in Hiroshima in 1945.

'My (school) uniform was blasted to shreds. The skin at the back of my head, my back, both hands and both legs had peeled off and was hanging down like rags.'

BBC, *Children at War*, 1989

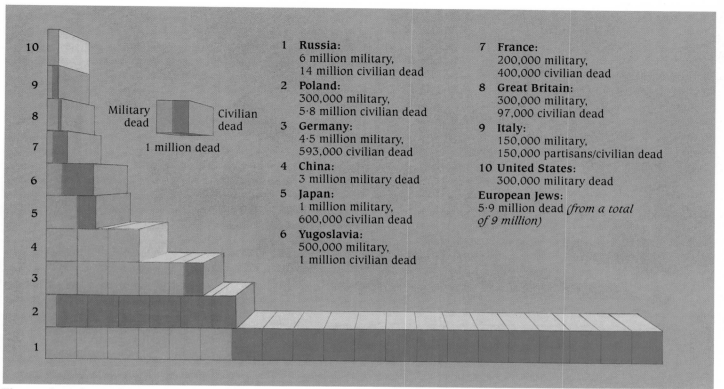

10		
9		
8	Military dead	Civilian dead
7	1 million dead	
6		
5		
4		
3		
2		
1		

1 **Russia:**
6 million military,
14 million civilian dead

2 **Poland:**
300,000 military,
5·8 million civilian dead

3 **Germany:**
4·5 million military,
593,000 civilian dead

4 **China:**
3 million military dead

5 **Japan:**
1 million military,
600,000 civilian dead

6 **Yugoslavia:**
500,000 military,
1 million civilian dead

7 **France:**
200,000 military,
400,000 civilian dead

8 **Great Britain:**
300,000 military,
97,000 civilian dead

9 **Italy:**
150,000 military,
150,000 partisans/civilian dead

10 **United States:**
300,000 military dead

European Jews:
5·9 million dead *(from a total of 9 million)*

The number of casualties suffered by nations in the Second World War.

Source 1

A jubilant American Serviceman in Piccadilly Circus celebrating the surrender of the Japanese.

1 a What different methods could the Americans have used to defeat Japan?
b For each method, explain its advantages and disadvantages.

2 There were many reasons why President Truman decided to drop the atom bomb. Put these reasons in order, starting with the most important.
◆ The Manhattan Project had cost a lot of money, so it would be a waste not to use the bomb.
◆ Invading Japan would cost too many Allied lives.
◆ No one in America or Britain much cared about how many Japanese were killed.
◆ Blockading Japan would take too long.
◆ Truman wanted to end the war with Japan quickly before the Russians joined in.
◆ A demonstration explosion would have been difficult to arrange and might not have persuaded the Japanese to surrender anyway.

3 a Do you think the Americans were *right* to use the atom bomb? (This is a difficult question to answer. You will need to think about it carefully and weigh all the evidence. Remember that there are very good arguments on both sides.)
b Do you think they needed to drop the *second* bomb?

14 Rebuilding Europe

It is difficult now to imagine the devastation in Europe in 1945. Whole cities were reduced to rubble, and the roads and railways were clogged up with refugees.

How did Europe recover from the war?

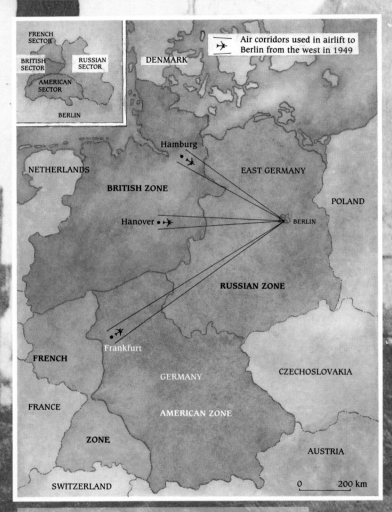

Air corridors used in airlift to Berlin from the west in 1949

FRENCH SECTOR
BRITISH SECTOR
RUSSIAN SECTOR
AMERICAN SECTOR
BERLIN

DENMARK

Hamburg

NETHERLANDS

BRITISH ZONE

EAST GERMANY

POLAND

Hanover

BERLIN

RUSSIAN ZONE

Frankfurt

FRENCH

CZECHOSLOVAKIA

GERMANY

FRANCE

AMERICAN ZONE

ZONE

AUSTRIA

SWITZERLAND

0   200 km

How Germany was divided by the Allies in 1945.

Germany

The German government had disappeared, so the Allies had to provide one of their own. Germany and Austria were divided up into four zones governed by the Allies: the USA, the Soviet Union, Britain and France. The two capital cities, Berlin and Vienna, were also divided into four sectors.

In their zone, the Russians began dismantling German factories, and sent machines back to Russia. The Americans and British tried to help the Germans rebuild the shattered homes which they themselves had bombed. In all the zones, people in important positions who had supported the Nazis were replaced with anti-Nazis.

Source A

People queueing for a bucket of water in devastated Berlin, 1945.

Dealing with the Nazis

Hitler, Goebbels and Himmler were all dead, but the Allies managed to capture a number of leading Nazis, including Hermann Goering. These people were charged with war crimes and tried at a special court at Nuremberg. The court watched films from concentration camps, and listened to witnesses. The Nazi leaders all said they were only obeying orders from other people. The court did not believe them, and most of them were sentenced to death.

Source B

The Nuremberg Trial. The surviving leaders of the Third Reich were put on trial for war crimes at the Nuremberg law courts. Twelve received death sentences.

The Allies made ordinary Germans come into the concentration camps to see for themselves what had been going on. Many Germans claimed this was the first they had known of the Holocaust.

The Marshall Plan

Europe was utterly devastated by the war and desperately needed

- new homes
- new factories
- new railways and roads.

In addition, millions of people had been killed or maimed during the war.

The American Secretary of State, General George C. Marshall, offered aid to European countries, as long as it was carefully planned and allocated.

Western countries accepted the offer eagerly, but the Russians were suspicious that Marshall Aid was a way of increasing American power in Europe, and refused it.

Thanks to Marshall Aid, western Europe recovered much more quickly than the areas under Russian control.

Refugees

The Nazis had torn people from their families all over Europe and transported them to nearly every part of the Continent. There were thousands of people in concentration camps in Germany and Poland. Children had been stolen from their parents and were with new families in Germany. Thousands of people had moved westwards to escape the Russians as they advanced. Not all of these refugees wanted to go home. Many preferred to start a new life in Britain or the United States.

Source D

Some of the millions of refugees forced from their homes during the war.

Sorting out who all these millions of people were, providing them with food and clothing, and working out where they would go (and where they would be allowed to go) was a huge task. The Red Cross did a lot of the work, and they were helped by a new organisation, the United Nations.

Britain

In Britain, people hoped that life would be better after the war. An economist, Sir William Beveridge, produced a report which suggested that

- the government should provide health care for everyone, from the cradle to the grave
- the government should provide unemployed people with help.

During the general election of 1945, the Labour Party promised to follow Beveridge's advice and Labour won by a large majority, defeating Churchill, who had led Britain throughout the war.

The new Labour Government

- introduced a National Health Service for everyone
- *nationalised* important industries, like the railways, electricity, gas and coal
- began to grant independence to Britain's colonies abroad.

1 Look back to Units 2 and 7 before you answer this question.
Why do you think:
a the Russians dismantled their zone of Germany, and
b the western Allies rebuilt theirs?

2 Why do you think the Allies tried the Nazis, instead of leaving it to the German courts?

3 The Soviet Foreign Minister called the Marshall Plan 'dollar imperialism'.
a What do you think he meant?
b Which aspect of the Marshall Plan do you think he had in mind?
c How might General Marshall have described his plan?

Source E
A Labour Party election poster of 1945.

A Third World War?

The war had not been over long before it began to look as if a new war might break out, this time between the western Allies and the Russians.

Why did the Allies and Russians fall out?

The United Nations

The old League of Nations had not been able to stop Hitler. After the Second World War, the Allies were determined to set up a stronger organisation, the United Nations Organisation, or UNO, now more often referred to as 'the UN'. The main aim of the UNO was to ensure that the world stayed at peace. The UNO was formally established on 24 October 1945 with 51 founder countries. The USA, the Soviet Union, Britain and China agreed the content of the United Nations Charter, which says:

- The UNO is not allowed to interfere in the internal affairs of any of its members.
- The UNO seeks co-operation on economic, cultural and humanitarian issues and human rights.
- The UNO aims to promote peace and co-operation between countries. It has the power to provide peace-keeping forces to settle disputes in war-torn countries.

Source A

The United Nations building, New York.

General Assembly

Sets the policies of the UN. All member states have one vote. Decisions need a two-thirds majority. Cannot do anything if the Security Council does not agree.

Security Council

Is responsible for maintaining peace and world security. There are five permanent members: the USA, the Soviet Union, Britain, France and China. Decisions must be unanimous – so a single member can block (*veto*) decisions.

Economic and Social Council

Co-ordinates the economic and social work of the Council. Some of its agencies are

- UNICEF: United Nations International Children's Emergency Fund, set up in 1946 to help refugee children.
- UNESCO: United Nations Educational, Scientific and Cultural Organisation.
- WHO: World Health Organisation.

International Court of Justice

Is based in The Hague, The Netherlands, to ensure that the Universal Declaration of Human Rights, which was adopted in 1948 and which details individual and social rights and freedom, is respected throughout the world.

Trusteeship Council

Promotes self-government in non-independent countries.

Secretariat

Administers the programmes and policies laid down by UN organisations.

The creation of the United Nations Organisation was the most significant development at the end of the Second World War. Its strength depended on the co-operation of the five Great Powers – the USA, the Soviet Union, Britain, France and China. But there was a rift between the Soviet Union and the United States, with support of the other Allies, which deepened into becoming almost a war – this became known as the Cold War – a war without fighting.

- What was the background to the rift between the Soviet Union and the United States?

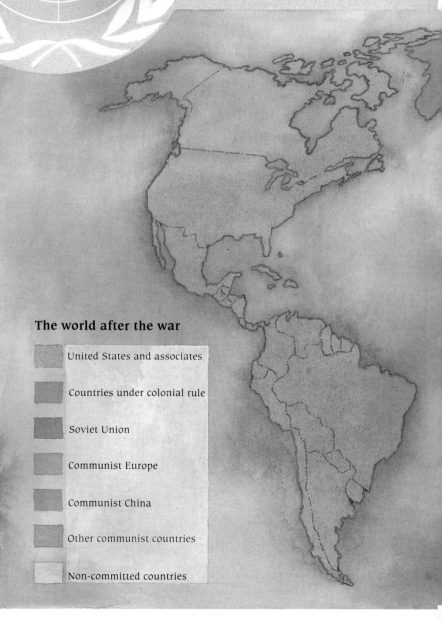

The world after the war

- United States and associates
- Countries under colonial rule
- Soviet Union
- Communist Europe
- Communist China
- Other communist countries
- Non-committed countries

The world after the end of the Second World War.

The Russians said:

- The United States, Britain and their allies have always wanted to destroy communism since 1919, when they attacked the Soviet Union in order to defeat the Russian Revolution.
- Britain and France did nothing to stop Hitler when they had the chance.
- The Russians did most of the fighting against Germany, while the British and Americans dithered about opening the Second Front.
- The Americans and British kept secrets from the Russians, even when they were all fighting on the same side.

The Russians felt that:

- the British and Americans are not to be trusted. We need to be defended against them.

The Americans said:

- Stalin has a long history of cruelty and mass murder, and there are no signs that he has changed.
- The Russians took control of eastern Europe by force and by cheating in elections, and they are keeping control by terror.
- All communists want to spread communism throughout the world, generally by force.
- The Russians are spying on everything that is going on in the west.

The Americans felt that:

- the Russians are not to be trusted. It is essential to stay strong enough to face up to them.

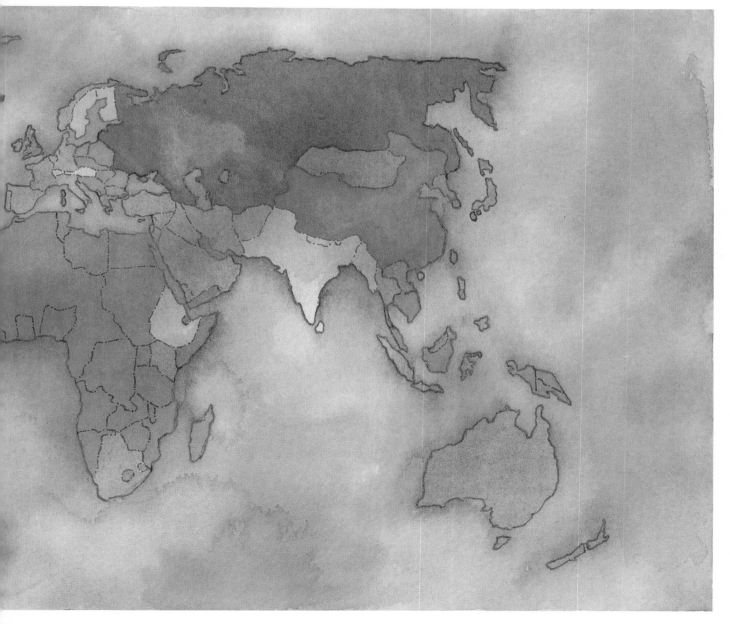

The Cold War
in the 1940s

1945
- Potsdam Conference – victorious leaders from the Soviet Union, the USA and Britain meet.
- Conference breaks down in deadlock when Truman refuses to allow Stalin to take more land.

1946
- Russians rig elections in eastern Europe to ensure massive majorities for communist parties.
- Winston Churchill attacks the Russians in a speech at Fulton, Missouri. He says that the Russians have set up an 'Iron Curtain' dividing Europe in two.

1947
- Truman announces the 'Truman Doctrine – to oppose the spread of communism anywhere in the world.

1948
- Communist coup in Czechoslovakia.
- Russians cut Berlin off from the west.

1949
- Communist revolution in China.
- Russians test their first atom bomb.
- West forms NATO – the North Atlantic Treaty Organisation.

Source B

Communist soldiers building the Berlin Wall in 1961. The divisions of the Cold War led directly to the construction of the wall.

The Berlin airlift

In June 1948 the Russians cut off all road and rail links between Berlin and the western zones. Stalin hoped to starve West Berlin into joining the Russian zone. But the Americans and British began a massive airlift to get vital supplies to Berlin. Thousands of aircraft took off each day until in May 1949 Stalin backed down and called off the blockade.

A year later, the Americans, British and French joined their zones of Germany together to form the Federal Republic of Germany, or 'West Germany' for short. The Russian zone became the German Democratic Republic, or 'East Germany'. Germany remained divided until 1990.

To many people, the late 1940s seemed like the 1930s again, as major powers seemed to be preparing for another war. The big difference was that by the end of the 1940s both sides had the atom bomb. Right until the Cold War ended in 1990, no one could know for certain that there would not be a Third World War.

---

1 Which of these statements are *facts*, and which are *opinions*?
◆ The UN was more effective than the old League of Nations.
◆ Thanks to their veto, the Security Council members could control anything that the UN did.
◆ The Russians wanted to control eastern Europe.
◆ The Americans wanted to control western Europe.

2 Look at what the Americans and the Russians said (page 89).

a What evidence is there to support each statement?

b Which side do you think was right?
You will have to look back through the whole book to answer these questions.

3 'Mankind has been disappointed that the Second World War was not immediately followed by the outbreak of universal peace. But this was not its object. The Second World War was fought to liberate peoples from Nazi and Japanese tyranny. In this it succeeded, at however high a price. Despite all the killing and destruction... the Second World War was a good war.'
A.J.P. Taylor, 1975
Do you agree with A.J.P. Taylor's summary? Explain your answer.

CONCLUSIONS

Although the Second World War ended many years ago it continues to affect life today.

How far is the modern world shaped by the events of the Second World War?

Divided Europe

Europe was divided in two by the Second World War, and differences between east and west remain to this day. The Soviet Union imposed communist governments on those countries of eastern Europe that they freed from Nazi control. It was not until 1989 that the people of eastern Europe were able to get rid of communism. By then, many of their economies were ruined and they were far behind western Europe in wealth and prosperity. The Baltic States, Estonia, Latvia and Lithuania declared themselves independent but when Yugoslavia did the same the country fell into a savage and bloody civil war. The bitter fighting between the different peoples of Yugoslavia during the Second World War had not been forgotten.

The Berlin Wall comes down.

Modern Germany. Like other German cities devastated by bombing, Frankfurt has been rebuilt since 1945.

92

Conflict in Palestine.

From the ashes

The defeated states of Germany and Japan were in ruins in 1945. In both countries there was an amazing comeback in the next half-century. Forbidden from building up large armies, the people of West Germany and Japan concentrated on rebuilding their economies. Within a few years they became two of the richest countries in the world.

Conflict in Palestine

One consequence of the war was a great wave of sympathy for Jewish people and an increase in Jewish migration to Palestine. This led to the founding of a Jewish state called Israel by the United Nations in 1948. Local Palestinian Arabs were angry about this and conflict between Jews and Arabs has continued to this day.

Modern Hiroshima. Surrounded by new offices, a building, which survived the atom bomb explosion in 1945, is kept as a memorial to those who died.

93

Attainment target grid

This grid is designed to indicate the varying emphases on attainment targets in the questions in each unit. It is not to be interpreted as a rigid framework, but as a simple device to help the teacher plan the study unit.

✘   some focus
✘✘   strong focus
✘✘✘ main focus

	AT1 a	AT1 b	AT1 c	AT2	AT3
1 Democracy and dictatorship			✘✘✘		
2 Germany prepares for war		✘✘✘	✘✘	✘✘	✘✘
3 Blitzkrieg		✘✘		✘✘	✘✘✘
4 Britain embattled		✘✘✘	✘✘	✘✘	
5 The Home Front in Britain			✘✘✘	✘✘	✘✘
6 Life under Hitler	✘		✘✘✘		✘✘
7 The Russian front	✘✘	✘✘✘	✘✘		✘
8 Pearl Harbor	✘	✘✘✘	✘✘		✘✘
9 The Holocaust	✘✘	✘✘	✘✘✘	✘✘	✘✘
10 Bombing		✘✘		✘✘✘	✘✘
11 D-Day	✘	✘✘	✘✘	✘✘✘	
12 Germany collapses		✘✘	✘✘✘		
13 The atom bomb		✘✘	✘✘✘		
14 Rebuilding Europe	✘✘✘	✘✘	✘✘	✘	✘
15 A Third World War?	✘✘	✘✘✘	✘✘	✘✘	✘

94

Index